SECURE IN THE EVERLASTING ARMS

SECURE
in the
EVERLASTING
ARMS

Elisabeth Elliot

SERVANT PUBLICATIONS
ANN ARBOR, MICHIGAN

Vine Books is an imprint of Servant Publications especially designed to serve evangelical Christians.

Servant Publications—Mission Statement
We are dedicated to publishing books that spread the gospel of Jesus Christ, help Christians to live in accordance with that gospel, promote renewal in the church, and bear witness to Christian unity.

Unless otherwise noted, Scripture quotes are from the New International Version. Verses marked (KJV) are from the King James Version. Verses marked (NEB) are from the New English Bible. Verses marked (PHILLIPS) are from the J.B. Phillips translation. Verses marked (CEV) are from the Contemporary English Version.

Published by Servant Publications
P.O. Box 8617
Ann Arbor, Michigan 48107
www.servantpub.com

Cover design: Paul Higdon, Minneapolis, Minn.

02 03 04 05 10 9 8 7 6 5 4 3 2 1

Printed in the United States of America
ISBN 1-56955-294-0

Library of Congress Cataloging-in-Publication Data

Elliot, Elisabeth.
   Secure in the everlasting arms / Elisabeth Elliot.
      p. cm.
   Includes bibliographical references.
   ISBN 1-56955-294-0 (alk. paper)
    1. Elliot, Elisabeth. 2. Christian biography—United States. I.
   Title.
   BR1725.E46 A3 2002
   277.3'0'2'092—dc21

                                                          2002000900

"The eternal God is your refuge, and underneath are the everlasting arms."

DEUTERONOMY 33:27

Contents

Introduction

This book is a collection of glimpses into my own lifelong adventure of living the Christian life, combined with faith-sustaining snippets from some of my favorite fellow pilgrims. All have appeared within the past ten years or so in *The Elisabeth Elliot Newsletter*, which has had a growing circulation for almost twenty years.

Some readers may be unfamiliar with the details of my life and thus become somewhat confused to read stories from such far-flung places as New Jersey, Florida, Alberta, Ecuador, China, India, Madagascar, and Massachusetts. Please know that, yes, I have had three husbands. And yes, I have been, over the years, a student, a missionary, a writer, a public speaker, and "just a housewife." I have spent a lot of time on airplanes and a lot of time pecking at the keyboard of a typewriter or computer.

But I have spent the most fruitful time sitting at the feet of the Lord Jesus, listening, reading, pouring out my heart, thinking, and learning. Perhaps because I am a slow student, God has had to teach me the same lessons many times. Of course, such frequent reviews have enabled me to write and speak better about some of the things I have learned, which I hope will benefit my readers and listeners.

Old age tends to make one reflective. Now the distant past enjoys renewed vibrancy in my recall, and it can be reviewed from the perspective of many years. Countless people have touched my life since the day I was born, seventy-five years ago, in Belgium.

I am told that when I was still an infant, the time came for my parents, who were missionaries, to return to the United States on furlough. Mother had carefully packed everything, had turned the key in the lock, and was standing on the sidewalk with a strong feeling that she had forgotten something. The Dutch maid was aware that Father had my older brother, three-year-old Philip, in tow, but she suggested that perhaps Mother might want to take along what she had left neatly on the bed upstairs—her five-month-old baby named Elisabeth.

While back in the U.S., my father, Philip E. Howard, Jr., was asked to join his father and uncle in the production of a weekly magazine called *The Sunday School Times*. So instead of returning to Belgium, he moved us to Philadelphia and later Moorestown, New Jersey.

When there were three of us children, we walked nearly a mile every day to school. I was fearful and worried that I would flunk the first grade (and perhaps every other grade straight through college!). Eventually there were six of us—four boys, two girls.

Our parents were relatively poor in the 30s, but we were always excited to have visitors to our home, particularly missionaries. I remember the visit of a famous English suffragette named Dame Christabel Pankhurst. My sister, Ginny—three or four years old—was utterly transfixed by this lady's brilliant red hair and painted eyebrows. We were all in agony awaiting the inevitable.

Sure enough, up spoke Ginny: "WHY does PANKABLE have RED eyebrows?" Somehow we managed to weather that disaster and others.

When I was a high school sophomore I went to Hampden

DuBose Academy, a Christian boarding school in Florida, and there I met my nemesis—an overpowering woman who set about at once making me over. I was terrified of Mrs. DuBose, who told me straight off that unless I pulled myself together and quit being shy I would flunk and be sent straight home. Somehow I managed to stick with it and graduate honorably.

I made it to Wheaton College in Illinois, where I found myself under the power of a fascinating old spinster professor who, on the very first day of class, started right in with a warning: "There will be *no* cutting of class, *no* postponing of assignments, and if you fall sick remember, that *sickness is an economic loss.*" Period. Case closed. Whew!

My major was classical Greek. There were forty-two men and two women in that class, plus the lovely young teacher who had graduated just three months earlier. She challenged me. She made me *love* Greek.

As I neared graduation I became aware that a certain gentleman was at times climbing over other students in class in order to sit by me. He was Jim Elliot, champion wrestler, my brother's roommate, and a man after God's own heart. He let me know he was interested but made it crystal clear that he was considering a life of celibacy. He was a year behind me.

I graduated and went to Prairie Bible Institute in Alberta, Canada, where I was taken under the wing of the most radiant, the most loving, the most heartwarming old saint, Mom Cunningham, who invited me to drop down to her little basement apartment at any time. Be assured that in many a bleak and howling prairie storm I made my way to that precious haven, where dear Mom would put on the kettle, open her Bible, and pray. When I went to Ecuador as a missionary she followed me with her prayers, always ending each letter with the Apostle Paul's words from Romans 15:13 (KJV): "Now the God of hope fill you with all joy and peace in believing, that ye may abound in hope, through the power of the Holy Ghost."

Five and a half years later, Jim Elliot and I married in Quito, Ecuador, and worked together with Quichua Indians in the eastern jungle. Our daughter Valerie was ten months old when Jim was killed, along with four other missionaries, by a tribe called the Aucas. I was able to go with my little three-year-old Valerie and live with those who had killed my husband and our missionary friends, and they have since learned who Jesus is. Some are carrying the good news to other jungle groups.

Returning to the U.S. in 1963, Valerie and I lived in New Hampshire until the man who became my second husband, Dr. Addison Leitch, wooed and won me. He moved us to Massachusetts, where he was a professor at Gordon-Conwell Theological Seminary. He was a good husband to me and stepfather to Valerie in her teen years, until he died of cancer. Lars Gren, a muscular Norwegian, is husband number three, and is in good health so far as I know today.

As I remember and re-tell these stories, I hope that you, reader of this book of "outtakes" of a life that has turned out to be rich with experiences, will adopt the same motto of faith that for thirteen years introduced my daily radio program, *Gateway to Joy:*

"Underneath are the Everlasting Arms."

ONE

❦

HIS EVERLASTING ARMS

Whatever My Lot

*J*ust after the Arab-Israeli war in 1967, I spent ten weeks in Jerusalem. One afternoon I was invited to have tea with Mrs. Bertha Spafford Vester, who had lived there all of her ninety-one years. A fascinating woman, she was the fifth daughter of Horatio Spafford, who wrote the song, "It Is Well with My Soul." The story of that beautiful hymn is familiar to many, but Mrs. Vester added details that were new to me.

The great Chicago fire of the 1870s caused Spafford, a wealthy businessman, to take stock of his life. Wanting to know Jesus better, he decided to sell everything and move to the land where He had walked. Shortly before the ship sailed, he was delayed by business, but took the family to New York. For some reason that he was unable to explain he had the purser change their cabin, moving them closer to the bow. He returned to Chicago to finish his business. Then came a telegram: SAVED ALONE. The ship had sunk. Mrs. Spafford had survived. Their four daughters had perished. Had they been in the cabin originally reserved amidships, all five would have drowned, for it was just there that the steamer had been struck by another vessel.

As we sipped tea and munched on Arab sweets, Mrs. Vester, who was not born until after the disaster, told me how her mother had described that terrible black night when she and her four little girls were flung into the cold sea. Frantically, she had tried to save them. Barely, she had been able to touch with her fingertips the hem of the little gown of one, but could not grasp it. She herself had been miraculously rescued as she floated unconscious on a piece of flotsam.

During Mr. Spafford's voyage to join his wife in France, the captain summoned him one day to the bridge. Pointing to his charts he explained that it was just here, where they were at that moment, that the other ship had gone down. Spafford returned to his cabin and wrote the hymn, which has comforted countless thousands.

When peace like a river attendeth my way,
When sorrows like sea-billows roll,
Whatever my lot, Thou hast taught me to say,
"It is well, it is well with my soul."

That word "lot" is not one we often use in quite that way. It means whatever happens, that which comes by the will of the powers that rule our destiny, a share, a portion, an assignment. When we draw lots, no human power controls which will be ours.

But Christians know that we are not at the mercy of chance. A loving hand, a great wisdom, and an omnipotent power rule our destiny. The government of all is on the mighty shoulders of Christ Himself, who sees all long before it happens. All is intended for our blessing. How different things look to us! Yet think of the faith of Horatio Spafford, suffering the loss of all his children, writing, "Whatever my lot, Thou hast taught me to say, 'It is well....'"

To love God is to love His will. That which He gives we receive. That which He takes we relinquish, "as glad to know ourselves in the hands of God as we should be sorry to be in our own," as Fénelon said. With what astonishment—of gladness or sadness—we receive some things! With what reluctance or delight we relinquish others! Yet we find that we can bear our own sufferings, while of others' sufferings we say, "That I could never bear!"

Jim, whose wife has cancer, wrote to me, "The assignment is *so* hard, but always there are the gracious gifts—the winks of heaven—a friend stopping by, a plumber coming at the perfect moment. Coincidences? Not to one with the eyes of faith."

God shields us from most of the things we fear, but when He chooses not to shield us, He unfailingly *allots* grace in the measure needed. It is for us to choose to receive or refuse it. Our joy or our misery will depend on that choice.

Shoes of Iron

*B*efore his death Moses blessed the twelve tribes of Israel. To Asher he said, "Thy shoes shall be iron and brass; and as thy days, so shall thy strength be" (Deuteronomy 33:25, KJV). How deeply the Lord set that promise into my heart on New Year's Day, 1973. My second husband, Addison Leitch, was to report on January 2 to the radiologist at Massachusetts General Hospital in Boston. His worst fear had come upon him. His first wife had died of cancer, his father had died of prostate cancer. Add had been diagnosed in October not only with cancer of the prostate but also with an unrelated but virulent cancer of the lip. As we came from the doctor's office on that day in 1972, he quoted Gray's Elegy: "The curfew tolls the knell of parting day."

New Year's Day is a good time to fix one's eyes on the only One who knows what the year is to hold. What is going to happen? What shall we do? Thomas à Kempis' *Imitation of Christ* has a lovely story about a monk who was anxious about his salvation. Christ spoke to him from the Cross: "If you knew that all was well, what would you today *do,* or *stop doing?* When you have found the answer, do it, or stop doing it." One must always get back to the practical and definite.

There is something marvelously sustaining about the knowledge that Thomas à Kempis and Samuel Rutherford and Amy Carmichael and Moses and the people of Israel and Mary and

Joseph and countless hosts of others have suffered and feared and trusted and been carried through in the same Everlasting Arms that hold us. And so, on that New Year's Day as I was imagining what that year might hold, I took that promise of "shoes of iron."

We shall be given shoes of iron. We shall find the unendurable endurable, the impossible possible. The natural processes of change and decay may be unexpectedly retarded to enable us to travel where no roads are visible, no replenishing available. The Lord is the one who travels every mile of the wilderness way as our leader, cheering us, supporting and supplying and fortifying us. Not all God's children, I suppose, have iron shoes—only the ones who need them! Lord, Thou knowest what we need.

I prayed then for four things: healing for Add, peace of heart for both of us, grace to help in time of need, and a fixed trust in God. The answer to the first was No. To the second it was, far more than I had had faith to expect, Yes. Grace and trust were always given according to my willingness to receive. There were many times "when my heart was grieved," as the psalmist wrote (Psalm 73). "I was senseless and ignorant; I was a brute beast before you. Yet I am always with you; you hold me by my right hand. You guide me with your counsel, and afterward you will take me into glory. Whom have I in heaven but you? And earth has nothing I desire besides you. My flesh and my heart may fail, but God is the strength of my heart and my portion forever."

My goal is God Himself—not joy, nor peace
Nor even blessing, but Himself, my God.
'Tis His to lead me there, not mine, but His—

"At any cost, dear Lord, by any road!"
So faith bounds forward to its goal in God
And love can trust her Lord to lead her there;
Upheld by Him, my soul is following hard,
Till God hath *full fulfilled* my deepest prayer.

No matter if the way be sometimes dark,
No matter though the cost be oft-times great,
He knoweth how I best shall reach the mark—
The way that leads to Him must needs be strait.

One thing I know, I cannot say Him nay;
One thing I do, I press towards my Lord:
My God my glory here from day to day,
And in the glory there my Great Reward.

(Source unknown)

To reread a journal that one wrote decades ago is a surprisingly faith-strengthening experience. There, amid all the exigencies and vicissitudes of life, one can trace the unbroken thread of the utter faithfulness of God—the measure of grace to help in time of need, unexpected kindness and help of many whom one knew, the physical strength needed to do what needed to be done, the spiritual renewal that came from the Father's continual pouring out of those mercies which He promised "endure forever," great mercies, and also some so small, so heartbreakingly sweet—my brother Tom coming often to sit with Add and to talk with me; Betty Lee sending me a bottle of bubblebath ("You must be tired—have a long, leisurely soak"); my dear friend Van calling to say, "It'll be all right, Bet. It'll be OK." (a contemporary version of Julian of Norwich: *All shall be well, and all shall be well, and all manner of thing shall be well*). C.S. Lewis speaks of being *happy* when his wife, Joy, was desperately ill and he himself *screaming* with the pain of osteoporosis—evidence that a brooding Providence is keeping all things under His control, as Gerard Manley Hopkins wrote in "The Golden Echo": "far with a fonder care kept than we could have kept it."

If today you look into the year ahead with deep forebodings, remember the God of Elisha. The king of Aram sent horses and chariots and a strong force to Dothan to capture him. Elisha's servant saw the king's chariots and horses surrounding the city and wailed, "Oh, my lord, what shall we do?"

"Don't be afraid," the prophet answered. "Those who are with us are more than those who are with them." Then he prayed, asking God to open the eyes of the servant. "He looked and saw the hills full of horses and chariots of fire all around Elisha" (2 Kings 6:17).

Ours is the same God. There is in Him no variableness or even a shadow caused by turning. If it's iron shoes we need, they will be provided. If it's a touch, a word, a gift from a friend, it will be given. If God sees that the mountain should be filled with horses and chariots, He'll fill it. Ask Him to open your eyes to His lovingkindness and tender mercies. Ask Him to help you to trust Him for tomorrow.

"Almighty God, we bless and praise Thee that we have wakened to the light of another earthly day; and now we will think of what a day should be. Our days are Thine, let them be spent for Thee. Our days are few, let them be spent with care. There are dark days behind us, forgive their sinfulness; there may be dark days before us, strengthen us for their trials. We pray Thee to shine on this day—the day which we may call our own. Lord, we go to our daily work; help us to take pleasure therein. Show us clearly what our duty is; help us to be faithful in doing it. Let all we do be well done, fit for Thine eye to see. Give us strength to do, patience to bear; let our courage never fail. When we cannot love our work, let us think of it as Thy task; and by our true love to Thee, make unlovely things shine in the light of Thy great love. Amen." (George Dawson, 1821-1876)

His Patient Silence

When Jesus was captured by the mob on the Mount of Olives He was taken to the house of the high priest where the guards mocked, beat, blindfolded Him, and demanded, "Prophesy! Who hit you?" Luke's account says that many other insulting things were said to Him, but not a word of reply is recorded. It was a solemn moment in His trial when, in all the confusion and cross-examination of witnesses, the high priest asked Jesus, "'Are you not going to answer? What is this testimony that these men are bringing against you?' But Jesus remained silent and gave no answer" (Mark 14:60-61).

What a tense, nearly heart-stopping moment it must have been—every eye fixed upon the Prisoner, every spectator waiting with bated breath for His reply. He spoke not a word. With the calm that flowed from unbroken communion with His Father, He heard the blasphemy, the insults, the ridicule. Despised and rejected by men, "He was oppressed and afflicted, yet He did not open His mouth; He was led like a lamb to the slaughter, and as a sheep before her shearers is silent, so He did not open His mouth" (Isaiah 53:7).

In Debrecen, Hungary, there is a museum built specifically to house Munkacsy's stunning triptych: Christ on the Pavement, Christ before Pilate, Christ on the Cross. Tears rushed to my eyes as we entered the immense room—three scenes, each filling an entire wall from ceiling to floor. The figures are life-size, the facial expressions of the spectators running the gamut from smugness and satanic glee to agonized love. In the first panel Christ stands erect and quiet, surrounded by a motley crowd. In the second, He has been stripped by His jeering captors and clothed in the purple robe. The crown of thorns has been jammed onto His brow. Still He stands, perfectly composed, as Pilate, with folded arms and knitted brow, wrestles with his soul-ripping dilemma. In the last, the face of Jesus is lifted to heaven, His mouth slightly open. Is it the tormented human cry of dereliction, "Why hast Thou forsaken Me?" or is it, perhaps, the final victory of spirit over flesh, His "Father, into Thy hands I commend My spirit"?

"For the transgression of my people he was stricken.... It was the Lord's will to crush him and cause him to suffer" (Isaiah 53:8, 10). *It was the Lord's will to crush Him.* Ought we not to meditate on that when we are tempted to ask why God allows *us* to suffer? We live in a fallen world, a world desperately in need of redemption. Jesus was not a stoic or indifferent or impervious. He bore our griefs. He carried our sorrows—bore them and carried them in a human body that felt every pain, heard every insult flung against Him, read the expression on every face, yet kept His perfect patience. "Shall I not drink the cup that the Father has given me?" (John 18:11).

Jim Elliot, at age twenty-two, wrote, "I think there is nothing so startling in all the graces of God as His quietness. When men have raged untruths in His Name, when they have used the assumed authority of the Son of God to put to death His real children, when they have with calloused heart twisted the Scriptures into fables and lies, when they have explained the order of His creation in unfounded theories while boasting the support of rational science, when they, using powers He grants them, claim universal autonomy and independence, He, this great silent God, says nothing! His tolerance and love for His creatures is such that, having spoken in Christ, in conscience, in code of law, He waits for men to leave off their bawling and turn for a moment to listen to His still, small voice of the Spirit. Now, after so long a time of restrained voice, bearing in Almighty meekness the blasphemies of His self destroying creatures, now, how shall it break upon the ears, the consciousness, hearts, and minds of reprobate men, the voice of One so long silent?

"It shall thunder with the force of offended righteousness; rage with lightning bolts upon the seared consciences; roar as the long-crouched lion upon dallying prey; leap upon, batter, destroy, and utterly consume the vain reasonings of proud humankind; ring as the battle shout of a strong, triumphant, victory-tasting warrior; strike terror and gravity to souls, more forcefully than tortured screams in the dead of night!

"O God, what shall be the first tones of Your voice again on earth? And what their effect? Wonder and fear, denizens of dust, for the Lord Himself shall descend from heaven with battle-cry, with the voice of the archangel, and the trumpet blast of God Himself made more terrible, if that could be, by the long suffering of His silence" (from the entry of November 29, 1949, in *The Journals of Jim Elliot*).

In the meantime, Heaven is silent. "Yes," writes Sir Robert Anderson, "but it is not the silence of callous indifference or helpless weakness; it is the silence of a great sabbatic rest, the silence of a peace which is absolute and profound—a silence which is the public pledge and proof that the way is open for the guiltiest of mankind to draw near to God."

"For God did not appoint us to suffer wrath but to receive salvation through our Lord Jesus Christ. He died for us so that, whether we are awake or asleep, we may live together with him" (1 Thessalonians 5:9-10).

What a thrilling hope—that we may live together with Him in heaven! But think of this—we may live together with Him *here* and *now,* a daily walking with Him who loved us and gave Himself for us.

A Dog's Thanksgiving

I remember fixing the wounded leg of my dog. There was some struggle and a hurt crying but he kept licking my hand. The hand of the one who was hurting him and the hand of the one who was healing him were the same, and his endurance of the one rested in his trust in the other. 'Out of the depths have I cried unto Thee, O Lord.'" (From *This Cup*, by Addison Leitch [my second husband, who died in 1973]).

There are many lessons for us in the mysterious animal world. Have we ears to hear, eyes to see, hearts to learn those sweet lessons?

Our Heavenly Healer often has to hurt us in order to heal us. We sometimes fail to recognize His mighty love in this, yet we are firmly held always in the Everlasting Arms. The dog's leg was hurting. Add's ministrations were as delicate as possible, yet they hurt too, and the loyal dog accepted them and thanked him with his eyes. Have we the humility to thank our Father for the gift of pain?

"No discipline seems pleasant at the time, but painful. Later on, however, it produces a harvest of righteousness and peace for those who have been trained by it" (Hebrews 12:11). Let us give thanks!

Praying and Acting

*T*here are many matters for prayer about which you and I can do nothing *except* pray. Those are the things we must leave entirely to God. There are other things that we ought always to lay before the Lord in prayer, *and* do something about. Some people are confused about this, wondering if to *do* something is a failure of faith or even a deliberate refusal to trust God.

Nehemiah, for example, while rebuilding the wall of Jerusalem, both prayed *and* posted a guard day and night to meet the threats of Sanballat and his crowd (Nehemiah 4:9). This was not in the least inimical to his confidence in God. To post a guard was no guarantee that Sanballat's plot would not succeed, but it was a reasonable human measure taken against it. Only God could control the final outcome, so to God Nehemiah went.

Hezekiah, at the point of death, wailed his lament to the Lord (Isaiah 38), turned his face to the wall and prayed, asking the Lord not for healing but only that he be remembered (2 Kings 20). The prophet Isaiah told him to apply a poultice of figs—a simple home remedy easily available. Was prayer not enough? Was it the poultice that healed him?

Prayer and action. Faith and obedience.

Paul prayed for the believers—earnest, eloquent, detailed prayers which he included in his epistles. But he did not leave it at that. He worked with all the strength God gave him to help them to sanctity. And then? Some grew saintly and others didn't.

Suppose we have prayed our hearts out over a matter, done all that was in our power to do, and then find that all was done in vain. Does our faith falter? Do we say prayer doesn't work? Has our obedience been futile?

What of the great prayer Jesus taught us to pray? It is for His kingdom and *His* will, yet we ought not to ask it unless we ourselves are prepared to cooperate. But how pitifully tiny our efforts seem, how ineffective, how absurd.

"We pray for peace in the world and yet we all know that wars and rumors of wars will go on until the end (our Lord Himself told us so).... We pray for the sick. What, exactly, (someone might urge) do we have in mind? That they will get well? Now? Do we suppose the hospitals will empty out because we have prayed?... To press such questions is to reduce the mystery of prayer to frivolity" (Thomas Howard, *If Your Mind Wanders at Mass*).

And yet we are taught to ask and taught to obey. Prayer and obedience.

A prayerful heart and an obedient heart will learn, very slowly and not without sorrow, to stake everything on God Himself. Is there evidence that His kingdom is on its way, that His will is being done on earth as it is in heaven? The day's news would not encourage us to think so. Let's remember Jesus' answer to the Pharisees who asked when the kingdom would come: "You cannot tell by observation when the kingdom of God comes. There will be no saying, 'Look, here it is!' or 'there it is!'; for in fact the kingdom of God is among you." (Luke 17:20, NEB).

Pray for the coming of the kingdom. Don't pray for it if you're not prepared to do something about it. To each of us is given a measured responsibility. Thy will and Thy kingdom, Lord, for Your Glory. My glad surrender to that holy will, my loving obedience, my prayers, my faith, my action, my daily taking up of the Cross—so may I say with Mary, "I am the Lord's servant; may it be to me as you have said."

"Lord, I know not what I ought to ask of Thee; Thou only knowest what I need: thou lovest me better than I know how to love myself. O Father! Give to Thy child that which he himself knows not how to ask. I dare not ask either for crosses or consolations; I simply present myself before Thee, I open my heart to Thee. Behold my needs which I know not myself; see and do according to thy tender mercy. Smite or heal; depress me or raise me up; I adore all Thy purposes without knowing them; I am silent; I offer myself in sacrifice; I yield myself to Thee; I would have no other desire than to accomplish Thy will. Teach me to pray. Pray thyself in me. Amen." (François de la Mothe Fénelon)

The Future Is Not Our Province

While a new year offers us a fresh start, it can also bring anxiety. Questions crowd into our minds. Will my job become redundant? Is God going to keep me single for another whole year? Where is that mate He's supposed to be bringing me? Where will the money come from for college, rent, clothes, food? Must I continue to suffer this person, this church, this handicap, this pain, this loneliness? We have a calming word in Psalm 138:8, "The Lord will fulfill his purpose for me; your love, O Lord, endures forever—do not abandon the works of your hands." That word stands. He will fulfill. His love endures. He will not abandon.

We are meddling with God's business when we let all manner of imaginings loose, predicting disaster, contemplating possibilities instead of following, one day at a time, God's plain and simple pathway. When we try to meet difficulties prematurely we have neither the light nor the strength for them yet. "As thy *days* so shall thy *strength* be" was Moses' blessing for Asher—in other words, your strength will equal your days. God knows how to apportion each one's strength according to that day's need, however great or small. The psalmist understood this when he wrote, "Lord, you have assigned me my portion and my cup; you have made my lot secure" (16:5).

What may be tomorrow's cross I never seek to find.
My father says, "Leave that to Me, and keep a quiet
  mind."

(Anonymous)

To lug into a new year all the baggage of past years would greatly impair our ability to concentrate on what our heavenly Father wants us to do. If there is someone we should forgive and learn to love, if there are debts which we have not paid, dishonesty we need to confess, an apology we must not postpone—or even a garage or closet that needs to be ransacked!—let us do what we ought to do *now*. Then we can say with Paul, "Not that I have already obtained all this, or have already been made perfect, but I press on to take hold of that for which Christ Jesus took hold of me. Brothers, I do not consider myself yet to have taken hold of it. But one thing I do: Forgetting what is behind and straining toward what is ahead, I press on toward the goal to win the prize for which God has called me heavenward in Christ Jesus" (Philippians 3:12-14). The Lord says, "Forget the former things; do not dwell on the past. See I am doing a new thing!" (Isaiah 43:18-19).

Oswald Chambers wrote, "Our yesterdays present irreparable things to us; it is true that we have lost opportunities which will never return, but God can transform this destructive anxiety into a constructive thoughtfulness for the future. Let the past sleep, but let it sleep on the bosom of Christ. Leave the Irreparable Past in His hands, and step out into the Irresistible Future with Him" (*My Utmost for His Highest,* Dec. 31).

Students often ask me how to find out what God's will is. I tell them that the will of God for them today is to study! That's not what they want to hear, but that is surely an important part of God's will for students. They must not cut classes, plagiarize on their papers, cheat on exams, treat the professor disrespectfully, or shirk their duty to their roommate. Faithfulness today is the best preparation for the demands of tomorrow. If my job is to wash the car or fire an employee (I'm thankful I've never had to do that!) or fish for lobsters *today*, the faithful performance of that humble task will enable me to accept tomorrow's assignment. When the young virgin Mary received an unexpected visitor she was greatly troubled and wondered what his greeting meant. The angel said, "Do not be afraid, Mary," and gave her the staggering piece of news that she was to give birth to Jesus, the Son of the Most High, whose kingdom would never end. What thoughts must have flashed through her mind as to the future—how to explain this, for example, to her fiancé Joseph?—but she did not give way to that fear. She said "Behold"—a word that means look upon regard, consider—"The handmaid of the Lord," putting herself instantly at His disposal, an act of unreserved self-donation and perfect surrender. She was attentive, willing, and ready to receive the Lord's word.

When Mary's story is told in Latin, the word is *Fiat*, a loaded word meaning "So be it," "Let it happen as You wish," or "May it be to me as You have said." And what of us? Are we assured that we are safe in the hands that hold the stars? Can we wholeheartedly surrender to God, leaving quietly with Him all the "what ifs" and "but what abouts"? Will we truthfully say to Him, "Anything You choose for me, Lord—to have to be, to do, or to suffer. I am at Your orders. I have no agenda of my own"? It comes down to *Trust* and *Obey*, "for there's no other way to be happy in Jesus," as the old gospel song goes. Our future may look fearfully intimidating, yet we can look up to the Engineer of the Universe, confident that nothing escapes His attention or slips out of the control of those strong hands. Remember the assurance of St. Julian of Norwich: *All shall be well, and all shall be well, and all manner of things shall be well.*

Angry At God?

My faith has been challenged; there has been bitterness in my heart toward God; I have been angry at Him for withholding this blessing from me."

The mail brings me many variations on this theme. Occasionally I am asked if I have ever been bitter or angry toward God because He took from me two much-loved husbands (He has mercifully given me yet a third—none of them sought after.) Unless my memory completely forsakes me I believe I can honestly answer *no*. Our adversary the devil has tempted me in many ways, but I don't think anger at God is one of them. I will try to explain why.

1. God is my heavenly *Father.* He loves me with an everlasting love. The proof of that is the Cross. First John 3:16 says, "This is how we know what love is: Jesus Christ laid down his life for us." As the hymn says, "Love so amazing, so divine, demands my soul, my life, my all."

2. Our heavenly Father wants nothing but the best for any of us, and only *He* knows what that is, for He is All-wise, the Omniscient. Even an earthly father wants the best for his child, but does not always know what that is.

3. God knows not only what we need but *when* we need it. When He withholds from us the one thing we feel sure would make us happy, it is well to remember His promise

that He will meet *all* our needs "according to his glorious riches in Christ Jesus" (Philippians 4:19). In other words, if we don't have it we don't need it—*now*. Perhaps He will give it next week, but that does not indicate indifference, forgetfulness, or poor timing. His time is always perfect.

4. Resentment makes us vulnerable to Satan, who is called the Destroyer. Think what a dangerous position we put ourselves in when we choose to be angry at God. Is there anywhere else for us to turn? In all the vast span of heaven or earth *there is no other refuge.* "God is our refuge and strength, an everpresent help in trouble. Therefore we will not fear" (Psalm 46:1-2). He is the Ruler of all. He's got the whole world in His hands. Shall we deliberately reject such a Refuge? Think of the danger in which we then place ourselves.

5. We have only this present moment. God does not usually give us previews of coming attractions. I can look back over many decades, remembering how worried I sometimes was, how bewildered at things God had permitted to happen, but now I see them all as a golden chain of mercies, gifts from a merciful Father who, like the father Jesus described, would never give his son a snake if he asked for a fish. What looks to us like a good thing might actually ruin us. How thankful I am for God's withholdings, for His unfailing faithfulness. Now, as I look forward to what may be left of my future, I think of John Greenleaf Whittier's beautiful lines:

I know not what the future hath of marvel or surprise,
Assured alone that life and death His mercy underlines.
And if my heart and flesh are weak to bear the untried pain,
The bruised reed He will not break, but strengthen and
    sustain.
No offering of my own I have, not works my faith to prove;
I can but give the gifts He gave, and please His love for
    love.
And so beside the silent sea I wait the muffled oar;
Nor harm from Him can come to me on ocean or on shore.
I know not where His island life their fronded palms in air,
I only know I cannot drift beyond His love and care.

Surely I never want to miss "islands" whose beauty I never dreamed of in those anxious times. I want to be able to honestly say, *Father, I trust You. Forgive me for being so foolish as to imagine that You have made a mistake. Help me to receive grace to keep a quiet heart, sure that I am, in this very moment, held in the Everlasting Arms.*

"Almighty God, give to Thy servant a meek and gentle spirit that may be slow to anger and easy to mercy and forgiveness. Give me a wise and constant heart, that I may never be moved to an intemperate anger for any injury that is done or offered. Lord, let me ever be courteous, and easy to be entreated; let me never fall into a peevish or contentious spirit, but follow peace with all men; offering forgiveness, inviting them by courtesies, ready to confess my own errors, apt to make amends, and desirous to be reconciled. Let no sickness or

cross accident, no employment or weariness make me angry or ungentle and discontented, or unthankful, or uneasy to them that minister to me, but in all things make me like unto the holy Jesus. Amen." (Jeremy Taylor, 1613-1667)

The Long Leisure of Eternity

In Maud Monahan's *Life and Letters of Janet Erskine Stuart*, she describes the long years of waiting on God and how He took nine years, "with all the long leisure of Eternity," to bring her to a guide who would "lead her soul out into paths of confidence and joy."

Stuart's words helped me to see that some of what I would have called my own stalling and obtuseness may have been the Lord's own timing. He makes us *wait.* He keeps us on purpose in the dark. He makes us walk when we want to run, sit still when we want to walk, for He has things to do in our souls that we are not interested in.

There have been times, on the other hand, when He wanted me to run but I only walked. Let us remember, however, that the Shepherd Himself sometimes makes us lie down. Some of the "delays" are His own choice for us, so we must not always chide ourselves when the pace is not what we thought it should be. We must learn to move according to the timetable of the Timeless One, and be at peace.

"My times are in thy hand" (Psalm 31:15, KJV). That is where I want to be, Father. May I rest in the sure knowledge that my hours and days are safely kept.

"Thou art good when Thou givest, when Thou takest away, when the sun shines upon me, when night gathers over me, Thou hast

loved me before the foundation of the world, and in love didst redeem my soul; Thou didst love me still, in spite of my hard heart, ingratitude, distrust. Thy goodness has been with me during another year leading me through a twisted wilderness, in retreat helping me to advance, when beaten back making sure headway. Thy goodness will be with me in the year ahead; I hoist sail and draw up anchor, with Thee as the blessed pilot of my future as of my past. I bless Thee that Thou hast veiled my eyes to the waters ahead. If Thou hast appointed storms of tribulation, Thou wilt be with me in them; if I have to pass through tempests of persecution and desolation, I shall not drown; if I am to die, I shall see Thy face the sooner; if a painful end is to be my lot, grant me grace that my faith fail not; if I am to be cast aside from the service I love, I can make no stipulation: only glorify Thyself in me whether in comfort or trial, as a chosen vessel meet always for Thy use." (from the *Valley of Vision: A Collection of Puritan Prayers and Devotions*, Arthur Bennett, ed.)

Two

*

Do the Next Thing

Called to Act

Among the treasures in a box of old family papers, I found a series of letters from a great-aunt who was serving as a hostess in a rest house in Virginia during World War I. She was a lady not used to working for a living, but her husband had dropped dead one day at the bank where he worked, and she had to find a way to support herself. She had opened her home to soldiers and sailors, many of whom were terribly homesick, some of them just back from the front with permanent disabilities. The wives and mothers of men who had been killed sometimes arrived at the door in the middle of the night, having just received the sorrowful news. My great-aunt Alice Sparhawk took care of them all.

Her letters to her brother "Chigsie" (Charles Gallaudet Trumbull) are full of cheerfulness and compassion. She was busy helping others every minute of the day and often late into the night. As I read her vivid and often humorous accounts of the daily routine, I remember the background of suffering against which she wrote—her own suffering (she could hardly bear to think of returning to the cheerful home where she and her husband, Jack, had lived) and that of so many others. But doing everyday duties for the sake of others saved her.

People who have themselves experienced both grief and fear know how alike those two things are. They know the restlessness and loss of appetite, the inability to concentrate, the inner silent wail that cannot be muffled, the feeling of being in a great lonely wilderness. Grief and fear are equally disabling, distracting, and destructive.

One may cry out in prayer and hear no answer. The heavens are brass. One may search Scripture in vain for some word of release and hope. There are many such words, but how frequently they seem only to mock us, and a voice whispers: "That's not meant for you. You're taking it out of context!" and no comforting word seems to reach us.

Faith, we know perfectly well, is what we need. We've simply got to exercise faith. But how to do that? How do we exercise anything at such a time?

"Pull yourself together!" With what?

"Cheer up!" How?

"Think positively!" But that is a neater trick than we are up to at the moment. We are paralyzed. Fear grips us tightly; grief disables us entirely. We have no heart.

At such a time I have been wonderfully calmed and strengthened by doing some simple duty. Nothing valiant or meritorious or spiritual at all—just something that needed to be done, like a bed to be freshly made or a kitchen floor to be scrubbed, one of those things that will never be noticed if you do it but will most certainly be noticed if you don't! Sometimes it takes everything you have to tackle the job, but it is surprising how strength comes.

Ezekiel was a man who witnessed many strange things and prophesied great cataclysms and splendors. He tells us little about himself, but in the twenty-fourth chapter of his book there is a powerful parenthesis: "The word of the Lord came to me:

'Son of man, with one blow, I am about to take away from you the delight of your eyes. Yet do not lament or weep or shed any tears. Groan quietly; do not mourn for the dead. Keep your turban fastened and your sandals on your feet; do not cover the lower part of your face or eat the customary food of mourners.' So I spoke to the people in the morning, and at evening my wife died. The next morning I did as I had been commanded" (Ezekiel 24:16-18).

Ponder those heart-rending words: "The next morning I did as I had been commanded"! God asked more of Ezekiel than any human being would dare to ask, but He knew His man. He was asking him to "put on a front," to act normally, not as a mourner, but to put on turban and shoes and eat his usual food. What extraordinary requirements to make of a man who has just lost the delight of his eyes! But Ezekiel had had plenty of practice in obedience and it was not his habit to bridle.

It sounds simple. But it is not easy. It was heroic, certainly. There are other incidents in the Bible where the doing of very ordinary things helped people out of deep trouble. When Paul was sailing as a prisoner to Italy and was about to be wrecked in the Adriatic Sea, everyone on board was terror-stricken. Sailors were trying to escape, the soldiers and centurion and captain were all sure they were doomed, and no one paid attention to Paul's assurances of faith in God. But when he suggested that they eat, and actually took bread himself and gave thanks for it, "they all were encouraged and ate some food…and when they had eaten enough, they lightened the ship, throwing out the wheat into the sea."

Terror had disabled and disoriented them. In their panic they thought only of desperate measures which might have saved a few. But where Paul's faith had had no effect on them, his common sense—"Let's eat"—restored them to their senses. Then they were able to see clearly what the next thing was to be done.

Emmi Bonhoeffer writes in *The Auschwitz Trials*, "From the very moment one feels called to act is born the strength to bear whatever horror one will feel or see. In some inexplicable way, terror loses its overwhelming power when it becomes a task that must be faced."

Thomas Carlyle said, "Doubt of any sort cannot be removed except by action." There is wonderful therapy in taking oneself by the scruff of the neck, getting up, and doing something. While you are doing, time passes quickly. Time itself will in some measure heal, and "light arises in the darkness"—slowly, it seems, but certainly.

I myself have been hauled out of the Slough of Despond by following the advice of the simple Saxon legend inscribed in an old English parsonage: "Doe the nexte thynge."

Many a questioning, many a fear,
Many a doubt hath its quieting here.
Moment by moment, let down from heaven,
Time, opportunity, guidance are given.
Fear not tomorrows, child of the King—
Trust them with Jesus. Do the next thing!

How to Prepare for Tomorrow

*J*esus, knowing exactly what awaited Him when He went up to Jerusalem, went. He had set His face to go there, and He moved steadily through the days, doing His Father's work of healing and peace with the same serenity that had always characterized His ministry. He told His disciples exactly what would happen and they understood none of it. On the way there, near Jericho, Jesus healed a blind man. Then He brought salvation to the house of Zaccheus. He wept over the city of Jerusalem, entered it, threw out the merchants from the temple, and carried on His daily teaching in the temple, until the Zero Hour arrived. Nothing dismayed or depressed Him enough to cause him to quit. The prospects of torture and death in no way hindered His day-by-day work that, as always, pleased the Father. This was His preparation: the faithful doing of the Will, one day at a time. Shall we, His children, not trust Him for our future?

Give me, O Lord,
   A steadfast heart,
   Which no unworthy affection
   May drag downwards;
Give me
   An unconquered heart,
   Which no tribulation

Can wear out;
Give me
An upright heart,
Which no unworthy purpose
May tempt aside.
Bestow on me also, O Lord my God,
Understanding to know You,
Diligence to seek You,
Wisdom to find You,
And a faithfulness
That may finally embrace You,
Through Jesus Christ our Lord.

(Thomas Aquinas)

Miss Andy

When the Tamiami Champion pulled into the Orlando railroad station one hot day in September 1941, a very tall, slim, dark-eyed lady in white was waiting for a new pupil of the Hampden DuBose Academy. She picked me out at once—a tall, very shy blonde girl of fourteen, wearing—of all things in *Florida* in *September*—a beige *felt* hat (we all wore hats in those days when we went anywhere), a blue *wool* dress and brown *suede* pumps.

"Hello!" said the lady. "You're Betty Howard and I'm Miss Andy. We're *so glad* you're here!"

She took my suitcase, led me to a station wagon, and drove me to the seedy old hotel in which the academy was then housed. This was the beginning of three years of boarding school—a school the likes of which no one would believe. There were about a hundred students, one third of whom were m.k.'s (missionary kids), one-third p.k.'s (preachers' kids), and one-third o.k.'s (ordinary kids). I was one of the last category. The school had been founded by Pierre Wilds DuBose, who had been a missionary kid in China and had a heart for those like him who were separated, often at an early age, from their parents. They made a home for all of us. All the teachers, I found, were unsalaried, living day and night in the dormitories during the school year and in cabins at a camp in North Carolina in the summer. Perhaps some occasionally were allowed a short visit home.

Miss Andy lived in the dormitory with us girls. Daily we saw lived out the high principle of Jesus' words in Matthew 25:40, "I tell you the truth, whatever you did for one of the least of these brothers of mine, you did for me." She, like the other teachers, showed us the meaning of sacrifice. She laid down her life for us. Love always means sacrifice.

Miss Andy was a woman with a gentle and quiet spirit, a radiant smile, total selflessness. She not only taught school. She planned the menus, did the shopping and countless other errands. When the school lost its only two paid employees, the cooks, it was Miss Andy who took over the task—not neglecting her teaching responsibilities. How was it possible? God knows.

Years later, in 1950, Dr. DuBose asked me to come to teach public speaking, taking the place for one semester of another teacher, his daughter, who was having a baby. I was Miss Andy's roommate during those months and was allowed to call her Jane. Far more intimately than I had had opportunity to observe before, I now saw, in humblest ways, what true sacrifice means. Jane was available to any and all who needed her at any time of the day or night. She and Dottie (Miss Hill) were often working on whatever needed to be worked on. If the phone rang at 3:00 A.M., it was Jane who answered it. If someone needed to be driven somewhere, Jane was the chauffeur. She had to be up and dressed by 7:00 A.M. or earlier, seven days a week.

She taught Bible classes not only to students but to Mrs. DuBose's church women. She prepared their elegant teas and the Christmas buffet supper—a lavish affair to which friends of the school were invited and students were trained (severely, before-hand) to serve.

Jane was—will always be—to me an icon of lovingkindness and quiet, hidden selflessness. On the last day of her life she taught school as she had done for fifty-nine years, and then cooked dinner. Like the woman who poured perfume on Jesus' head, she did what she could. As I review the life of my beloved Jane it seems to me that she did what she couldn't! But we know from whence came her help—the Lord who made heaven and earth, the Lord who promised "As thy days, so shall thy strength be."

How May I Serve Christ Today?

A hymn by John Keble (1822) has been a great help to me as I seek to make all that I do an offering to the Lord. A day at home always holds housework, correspondence, and some ways in which I can serve my husband. This hymn has enriched my understanding of Paul's rule for Christian households, found in Colossians 3:18-24. He speaks to wives, husbands, children, fathers, and slaves. The work of a slave was surely the most menial and thankless, but what changed aspect that work would hold if he saw it as service to the Lord Himself!

"Slaves, obey your earthly masters in everything; and do it, not only when their eye is on you and to win their favor, but with sincerity of heart and reverence for the Lord. Whatever you do, work at it with all your heart, as working for the Lord, not for men, since you know that you will receive an inheritance from the Lord as a reward. It is the Lord Christ you are serving (Colossians 3:22-24)."

All work, if offered to Him, is transformed. It is not secular but sacred, sanctified in the glad offering. There was once an anchoress (a female hermit) in England who had renounced the world in order to live in seclusion. She was enclosed for life inside a little cell built into the church wall. There was a very small window opening to the street where passersby often paused, asking for her prayer and counsel. This, most of us would agree, was "spiritual" work. But it came to pass that the route of the main thoroughfare was changed and few came by to seek her help. The neighborhood children, however, found her and began to bring to her their broken toys. Gladly she mended the toys, seeing this as the Lord's new assignment—as sanctified as was her former work.

Is there not a very important lesson for all of us here? In the very place where God has put us, whatever its limitations, whatever kind of work it may be, we may indeed serve the Lord Christ. The following are a few of the stanzas of Keble's hymn. Think about them while you peel a carrot, drive a truck, listen to a bore, receive criticism, or do any other task that seems odious:

New every morning is the love
Our waking and uprising prove;
Through sleep darkness safely brought,
Restored to like and power of thought.

If on our daily course our mind
Be set to hallow all we find,
New treasures still, of countless price,
God will provide for sacrifice.

The trivial round, the common task,
Will furnish all we ought to ask;
Room to deny ourselves—a road
To bring us daily nearer God.

"Go in all simplicity; do not be anxious to win a quiet mind, and it will be all the quieter. Do not examine so closely into the progress of your soul. Do not crave so much to be perfect, but let your spiritual life be formed by your duties, and by the actions which are called forth by circumstances. Do not take overmuch thought for tomorrow. God, who has led you safely on so far, will lead you on to the end. Be altogether at rest in the loving holy confidence which you ought to have in His heavenly Providence." (St. Francis de Sales)

What to Do Next

*E*very summer I go into the attic and clear out a few more things. Last summer I delved into the box containing all the letters I had ever written to my parents, beginning in 1941 when I went away to boarding school. Mother had carefully kept in chronological order the letters from all six of her "bairns" until 1982 when her mind lost its keen edge. It seemed rather foolish to hold on to things if one was never going to look at them again, so I pulled out the file that describes a crucial segment of my life, my first widowhood after my first husband, Jim Elliot, was killed by Auca Indians in Ecuador on January 8, 1956.

Valerie was ten months old. As the only missionary on our jungle station at that time I was strongly tempted to fear. Would I be able to carry on without Jim, who had been running the station, building our house, managing the Quichua workers, teaching the new believers, working with me on Bible translation? Where to begin? What to do next?

Very likely some of you are asking yourselves this last question. An array of things you had meant to do last year were not done. Things you prayed earnestly for last year did not happen as hoped. People you counted on fell by the wayside. All sorts of unwanted events took place. Matters that simply must be dealt with this year stare you in the face. I can't think of a better time to review that tremendous eleventh chapter of Hebrews. The word *faith* occurs twenty-eight times.

The ancients were commended for a solid faith full of hope and based on a strong certainty. We might take an invaluable lesson from them: *Obedience to God is our job. The results of that obedience are God's.*

Did Noah have private misgivings about constructing that preposterous vessel? I should think he had, but his trust outweighed his doubts. He simply obeyed.

When the Lord told Abraham to leave his country, his people, and his father's household, was he astounded? Fearful? Rebellious? He obeyed and went, not knowing where he was going. When he was called to make the supreme sacrifice of his son Isaac, did his heart leap from his chest? He reasoned that God could (and perhaps might) raise the dead. He got up early in the morning, saddled his donkey, took two servants and his son, cut enough wood for a burnt offering, and set out on a three-day journey, every step of which must have been agony. When all was prepared (including his heart, surely), he raised the knife—his trust and obedience perfected—whereupon God sent an angel with a message, "Because you have not withheld your son, your only son, I will surely bless you ... because you have obeyed me."

Moses chose to be ill-treated along with the people of God rather than to enjoy the pleasures of sin for a short time. Following the stories of more heroes named in Hebrews 11 are unnamed heroes who were tortured, jeered at, flogged, chained, imprisoned, stoned, sawn in two (think about that one!)—and on and on.

Verses 39 and 40: "These were all commended for their faith, yet none of them received what had been promised. God had planned something better for us so that *only together with us* would they be made perfect." That stuns me. Their perfection awaits ours. Their names are to be linked with yours and mine. Yours, Tom, Dick, and Harry! And yours, Elisabeth.

So what shall we do? The answer is given:

> Therefore, since we are surrounded by such a great cloud of witnesses, let us throw off everything that hinders and the sin that so easily entangles, and let us run with perseverance the race marked out for us. Let us fix our eyes on Jesus, the author and perfecter of our faith, who for the joy set before him endured the cross, scorning its shame, and sat down at the right hand of the throne of God. Consider him who endured such opposition from sinful men, so that you will not grow weary and lose heart.
>
> HEBREWS 12:1-3

Are we aware that there is a race marked out for each of us? How determinedly will we run? If you are one of those who has not received what was promised, will you trust God anyway?

Help us, Lord, to get rid of whatever weighs us down, to keep our eyes fixed on Jesus, "who for the joy set before him endured the cross."

In what form shall we expect our crosses to be presented to us in the year to come? Something heroic, perhaps? Dramatic? Spectacular? Very unlikely for most of us, I think. John Henry Newman (1801-1890) wrote, "To take up the cross of Christ is no great action done once for all; it consists in the continual practice of small duties which are distasteful to us." Perhaps it is simply one of those small duties, gladly tackled, that will point to what to do next. If the assignment is a fearful one, take courage from that valiant and tested old Scot named Samuel Rutherford (1600-1661): "For some it is 'Down crosses and up umbrellas!' but I am persuaded that we must take heaven with the wind and the rain in our faces."

Praise of the Lamb

Revelation 5 speaks of everything created joining in the praise of the Lamb. Their voices will be quite a chorus of bleating, quacking, roaring, squeaking, growling, chirping, whistling, grunting, cackling, mooing, mewing, trumpeting, snarling, peeping, hissing, chattering, cawing, trilling, ratcheting, squealing, humming, cooing, screeching, howling, baying, neighing, whinnying, whickering, braying, bellowing, gobbling, crowing, singing, barking, and croaking. (I wonder how Noah's wife put up with all that?) But at last, when everything that has breath shall praise the Lord, I think the noise will be interpreted as "Holy, holy, holy! Worthy is the Lamb!"

I went to a Florida beach early one morning. Starlight. Warm tropical breeze. Solitude. Sighing of a gentle surf at low tide. Sat on a sand dune to watch the sun rise, read the Bible, and prayed. Listened to ground-doves, mockingbirds, a cardinal. Watched tiny crabs, looking like delicate stagecoaches with two footmen atop. A grey heron stalked solemnly on the sand, gobbling them. A pelican crash-landed in the waves. A fishing boat went by. A jet plane headed north. Found a strange dead fish, eighteen inches long, like a thick bag with "tire treads" on its underside, a big rubbery mouth, huge eyes.

"How many are your works, O Lord! In wisdom you made them all; the earth is full of your creatures. There is the sea, vast and spacious, teeming with creatures beyond number—living things both large and small" (Psalm 104:24-25).

I came upon many turtle tracks. When the sea turtle makes her way out of the sea up onto dry sand to lay her eggs, she is alone. She chooses the exact time and tide, the right distance from the high water mark, the depth she must dig. No one instructs her—no one, that is, but her Maker. And what communion do they hold there in the moonlight? Who gives her strength to bear the load of up to 250 eggs while at the same time she is digging a deep hole to deposit them? Who teaches her that she must cover the eggs with sand and smooth it so that the nest is not easily detectable? Who leads her back into the deeps? She obeys Him, thus joining the throng who glorify Him day and night.

Came home to nothing but bad news on TV—many things tempt me to worry. But then I remembered that we are always under "the blessed controller of *all* things" (1 Timothy 6:15, PHILLIPS). He has clearly told us that we are not to worry about anything whatever. We are to remember the birds—grounddoves, mockingbirds, cardinals, pelicans, and herons among countless others—fed by a heavenly Father, the lilies that toil not, even the grass which is clothed by God. Often I have been comforted by the reminder that my Heavenly Father knows exactly what I need and has told me to "seek his kingdom and his righteousness, and all these things will be given to you as well. Therefore do not worry about tomorrow, for tomorrow will worry about itself. Each day has enough trouble of its own" (Matthew 6:33-34).

The Consolation of Obedience

*E*arly one Sunday morning in the mountains of North Carolina a group of conference speakers met as planned for prayer, but heard a shocking announcement. The son-in-law of that morning's speaker had been murdered in South America. There were many expressions of grief and sympathy, of course, and it was agreed almost unanimously that another speaker should be found for the worship service. "No," said the scheduled speaker quietly. He wanted to carry out his responsibility. Objections, consternation, discussions followed.

"But I want to do it," said the man.

Surely it would not be right to expect him to do this, not after hearing such terrible news. All would wish to excuse him. All would understand. When the men had had their say, I ventured to suggest that perhaps there was one thing they did not understand—that in times of deepest suffering it is the faithful carrying out of ordinary duties that brings the greatest consolation. I had found it so, as have many others. The man delivered his message—a deepened and more powerful one.

I had seen an example of this in Marj Saint. Her daily job was to maintain constant radio contact with her husband, Nate, a jungle pilot. When he and four missionaries, including my first husband, went into dangerous territory in Ecuador in 1956 Marj lost contact with her husband for the first time in all the years he had been flying. Through the suspense of four days we watched as she sat calmly, hour after anguished hour, by that short wave radio. Headphones on, notepad ready, she maintained contact with another jungle pilot, with an American air rescue party from Panama, with reporters from Quito and the U.S., and with the search party comprised of Quichua Indians, missionaries, and Ecuadorian soldiers. She had a few other things to think about as well: Her three children, us four wives, and our children who were all staying in her house, not to mention the people who poured in from all over, wanting to help. When one missionary lady offered "a shoulder to cry on," Marj thanked her and said she hoped she would not need it. God was her mighty fortress and her routine work was real consolation. There was no turning away from her duties or from people simply because her own heart was sick and sore. She knew the truth of Romans 8:35-39:

> Who shall separate us from the love of Christ?
> Shall trouble or hardship or persecution or famine or nakedness or danger or sword? As it is written:
> "For your sake we face death all day long;
> we are considered as sheep to be slaughtered."
> No, in all these things we are more than conquerors through him who loved us. For I am convinced that neither ... height nor depth, nor anything else in all creation, will be able to separate us from the love of God that is in Christ Jesus our Lord.

I remember the consolation I had found in going about my

work in Shandia when Jim died. There was twice as much to do as there had been when there were two of us. In my journal of November 1973, about two months after the death of my second husband, Addison Leitch, I wrote:

"I find that routine is the best support for my soul. I can function with almost my customary efficiency and concentration, so long as I operate by habit—the sameness, ordinariness, and necessity are comforting. It is in the interruption of routine that I find myself beginning to disintegrate and turn inward. This is hazardous, and I have to take the reins firmly and say *giddap!*"

It was the old watchword, "Do The Next Thing." But how to know which, of all pressing concerns, is the next thing? As usual, George MacDonald has an answer:

Your next duty is just to determine what your next duty is. Is there nothing you neglect? Is there nothing you know you ought not to do? You would know your duty if you thought in earnest about it, and were not ambitious of great things."

"Ah, then," responded she, "I suppose it is something very commonplace, which will make life more dreary than ever. That cannot help me."

"It will if it be as dreary as reading the newspapers to an old deaf aunt. It will soon lead you to something more. Your duty will begin to comfort you at once, but will at length open the unknown fountain of life in your heart.

It is a principle of the spiritual life discovered by many. Here is John Keble's version:

When sorrow all our heart would ask,
   We need not shun our daily task,
And hide ourselves for calm;
The herbs we seek to heal our woe
Familiar by the pathway grow,
   Our common air is balm.

What Love Does

*E*verything is an affair of the spirit. If eating and drinking can be done "to the glory of God" (1 Corinthians 10:31, KJV) so can everything else. For those who long to follow Christ, "the performance of smaller duties, yes even of the smallest, will do more to give us temporary repose ... than the greatest joys that can come to use from any other quarter" (George MacDonald).

At a conference where I was speaking about the little sacrifices of love I suggested that if, for example, your husband drops his clothes on the floor and leaves them there, you might instead of nagging (your views on the subject have been well-known to him for a long time!) simply pick them up. This sort of suggestion does not go over well these days—we're terrified of being "walked on," or becoming "co-dependent" or "enablers." One woman's questions following that talk were:

1. Why shouldn't my husband *change* and quit dropping his clothes?
2. If he doesn't, how do I handle the resentment I feel?

The first answer is simple: Of course he should change, but you can't make him! God knows you've tried. It's time to leave him to God. (I was not talking to husbands!)

The second question pierces to the heart of things: The resentment—my heart, my attitude toward the man—reveals

73

my attitude toward Jesus Himself, for what I do to one of His brothers, I do to Him—alas!

I greatly value Question and Answer sessions, hoping to clarify the application to individual lives of the principles I try to set forth. But having been at this a good number of years, I am more and more aware of the difficulty of helping people to turn their eyes to *Jesus*. The world is, as Wordsworth put it, *too much with us*. Has a husband's careless habit anything to do with my relationship to Jesus? Yes, everything to do with it.

As I reminded my daughter Valerie (in the book I wrote as a wedding present to her, *Let Me Be A Woman*), you marry a sinner. There simply isn't anything else to marry. So the husband sins against the wife and—let us wives not forget—he, too married a sinner. If he sins in being thoughtless and my reaction is sinful, two wrongs don't make a right.

Most questions about relationships can be answered quite simply if we ask ourselves this question: What does *love* do?

Let me start with my love for God. Loving Him means the thankful acceptance of all things that His love has appointed. We learn to love Him as we learn to "frame our heart to the burden," as Samuel Rutherford said. Clothes on the floor constitute, at worst, a small "burden." This, if not accepted as soon as we find that we are not in a position to change it, becomes an irritation, which then becomes resentment, which becomes real anger and, eventually, along with all the irritation not accepted for the love of God, becomes full-dressed hatred. "Whoever hates his brother is in the darkness and walks around in the darkness; he does not know where he is going, because the darkness has blinded him"

(1 John 2:11). No wonder we lose our way. No wonder we are baffled. Darkness descends because we do not ask the Lord to teach us love.

Surely the questioner would protest that she does not hate her husband. But she certainly hates what he does, and marriages break up when "small" things accumulate and resentments build. Love is the intention of unity. Resentment is the destroyer of unity.

John S. Dwight (1813-93) said, "Rest is the fitting of self to its sphere." If in my "sphere" I find things out of place through someone else's fault this is my opportunity to *fit* myself, to *give* a little, to do the small thing that should have been done by the other. Love is very patient, very kind, never rude, never selfish. And it's amazing what rest comes from the gentle fitting of self to its sphere.

Now as to the "handling" of resentment? Again, turn your eyes upon Jesus. Had He good reason to be resentful? Did people treat Him with respect, believe His words, trust His judgments, follow His leading, love and obey Him? Think on these powerful words:

If you suffer for doing good and you endure it, this is commendable before God. To this you were called, because Christ suffered for you, leaving you an example, that you should follow in his steps. "He committed no sin, and no deceit was found in his mouth." When they hurled their insults at him, he did not retaliate; when he suffered, he made no threats. Instead, he entrusted himself to him who judges justly.... By his wounds you have been healed.

1 PETER 2:20-24

In her thought-provoking little book called *If,* Amy Carmichael writes: "If I am soft to myself and slide comfortably into the vice of self-pity and self-sympathy; if I do not by the grace of God practice fortitude, then I know nothing of Calvary love."

Some things may legitimately be alleviated, others necessarily endured. May we be wise enough to know the difference.

THREE

❧

DAILY FAITH

Not Mad at God

*J*im O'Donell was a very ambitious and successful business-man who described himself as self-centered and indifferent to spiritual things until he met Christ through a man who rode the same commuter train to Boston.

With a desire to be a *servant* Jim gave up his work in Boston and moved with his wife Lizzie to Huntington, Indiana to teach in a small Christian college. Not many months later they learned that Lizzie had breast cancer, "dangerous, virulent, and advanced." He gave me permission to quote from his letter, a very unusual one, I think:

How could something so serious strike so rapidly? And selfishly I ask, "Why sweet Lizzie?"... We believe strongly in the power of prayer. We are not mad at God. (It is God who has given me Lizzie for the past twenty-eight years.) Our faith has not been shaken, though this is a time of severe testing.... We must learn how to be faithful people in this new assign-ment, one we certainly never would have asked for but one which can still serve us, bless us, our Creator, and others.

Yes there is fear; there is sadness, there is a whole new vocabulary we are coming to know, one we never would have wanted to know anything about. There are lots of tears. But there have been extraordinary blessings amid the darkness....

We don't believe this is an accident, and we don't believe this is not "of God." We live in a fallen world, where all of us—and creation in general—fall short, because of sin, of what God intended for us; and illness and crime and cruelty are just reminders of that "fallenness." We trust in God's sovereignty over this world and for our lives amid this sickness. God can heal. But we also trust that even serious illness can serve God's good and holy purposes to arouse love and care in others, to turn our trust from ourselves to Him, and maybe spur some to reflect on what truly is important in life.

His letter ends with eight wonderful verses about suffering in 2 Corinthians 1:3-11:

Praise be to the God and Father of our Lord Jesus Christ, the Father of compassion and the God of all comfort, who comforts us in all our troubles, so that we can comfort those in any trouble with the comfort we ourselves have received from God. For just as the sufferings of Christ flow over into our lives, so also through Christ our comfort overflows. If we are distressed, it is for your comfort and salvation; if we are comforted, it is for your comfort, which produces in you patient endurance of the same sufferings we suffer. And our hope for you is firm, because we know that just as you share in our sufferings, so also you share in our comfort.

We do not want you to be uninformed, brothers, about

the hardships we suffered in the province of Asia. We were under great pressure, far beyond our ability to endure, so that we despaired even of life. Indeed, in our hearts we felt the sentence of death. But this happened that we might not rely on ourselves but on God, who raises the dead. He has delivered us from such a deadly peril, and he will deliver us. On him we have set our hope that he will continue to deliver us as you help us by your prayers. Then many will give thanks on our behalf for the gracious favor granted us in answer to the prayers of many.

Jim told me in a later note that he was kept from fear and despair by the thought that God has specific assignments for us during our lives. "He makes our assignments ... a wonderful teaching planted in this growing soul." Psalm 16:5 is an expression of this truth.

C.S. Lewis said that God whispers to us in our joys, speaks to us in our conscience, and *shouts* to us in our pain.

Perfect Peace

*A*my Carmichael gives a beautiful illustration from nature of perfect peace. The sun bird, one of the tiniest of birds, a native of India, builds a pendant nest, hanging by four frail threads, generally from a spray of valaris. It is a delicate work of art, with its roof and tiny porch, which a splash of water or a child's touch might destroy. She tells how she saw a little sun bird building such a nest just before the monsoon season, and felt that for once bird wisdom had failed—for how could such a delicate structure, in such an exposed situation, weather the winds and torrential rains? The monsoon broke and from her window she watched the nest swaying with the branches in the wind. Then she perceived that the nest had been so placed that the leaves immediately above it formed little gutters which carried the water away from the nest. There sat the sun bird, with its tiny head resting on her little porch, and whenever a drop of water fell on her long, curved beak, she sucked it in as if it were nectar. The storms raged furiously, but the sun bird sat, quiet and unafraid, hatching her tiny eggs.

"We have a more substantial rest for head and heart than the sun bird's porch! We have the promises of God. They are enough, however terrifying the storm."

Beneath the cross of Jesus I fain would take my stand,
The shadow of a mighty rock within a weary land;

A home within the wilderness, a rest upon the way,
From the burning of the noontide heat, and the burden
  of the day.

I take, O Cross, thy shadow for my abiding place.
I ask no other sunshine than the sunshine of His face,
Content to let the world go by, to know no gain or
  loss,
My sinful self, my only shame; my glory all the Cross.

(Elizabeth Clephane)

The Test of My Love for God

hat is the true test? We can sing about it, talk about it, preach about it, write poetry about it, pray about it. But Jesus spelled out the acid test: "If you love me, you will obey what I command. Whoever has my commands and obeys them, he is the one who loves me" (John 14:15, 21). Obedience is the valid proof.

If my reaction to one who has done me wrong is less than a loving forgiveness, I simply cannot claim to love God. When we pray, "Forgive us our trespasses as *we forgive* those who trespass against *us*" we are telling God that we will receive from him exactly the measure of forgiveness we have willingly offered to the trespasser. Will that be enough? Will that cover our trespasses against our Savior? No, it won't, for Jesus said, "If you do not forgive men their sins, your Father will not forgive your sins." This is the only petition in the Lord's Prayer with a condition. Forgive me as I have forgiven that person who has not asked for forgiveness, that person who has ruined my marriage or my business or my chance to succeed, that person who goes on blithely as though he had done nothing wrong and couldn't care less. Will I erect a wall between him and me? Then I do the same to God. It's the same wall. Therefore I cannot obtain forgiveness. We must admit guilt—rather than hide in "an aristocracy of self-righteousness." To be a Christian means rising out of our guilt and being transformed by God's forgiveness.

Watchman Nee told the story of a Chinese farmer who, as soon as he became a believer, underwent a severe test to the validity of his faith. A daily task was to pump water by hand up the steep hillside. A neighbor breached the retaining bank and ran the farmer's water onto his own garden. "It is not righteous!" said the farmer to the elders in the church. "What does a Christian do in such a case?" The elders knelt with him in prayer, then thought of Jesus' words, "If someone take your coat, give him your cloak also." "If we do only the 'right' thing," said the elders, "we are unprofitable servants. We must go beyond what is merely right."

The next day the farmer went to work at his treadmill, pumping water for his neighbor's two strips of wet land below. He then spent the afternoon laboriously pumping water for his own garden. The neighbor, of course, was dumbfounded. He questioned the Christian and it was not long before he too was drinking the Water of Life.

A lady who heard this story said to me, "I know why God had me come here today. I've had years of contention with a neighbor who had been gradually encroaching on my property. I've been furious with him, and no amount of reason has helped the situation. Today I learned that I do not have to expect reason! I am going to deed him the property he has appropriated. How simple! And what a relief!"

"We know that we have passed from death to life, because we love our brothers. Anyone who does not love remains in death" (1 John 3:13). No need to remain in death. Just let go of the bitterness.

"Oh, how many times we can most of us remember when we

would gladly have made any compromise with our consciences, would gladly have made the most costly sacrifices to God, if He would only have excused us from this duty of loving, of which our nature seemed utterly incapable. It is far easier to feel kindly, to act kindly, toward those with whom we are seldom brought into contact, whose tempers and prejudices do not rub against ours, whose interests do not clash with ours, than to keep up an habitual, steady, self-sacrificing love towards those whose weaknesses and faults are always forcing themselves upon us, and are stirring up our own. A man may pass good muster as a philanthropist who makes but a poor master to his servants, or father to his children." (F.D. Maurice, 1805-1872)

"Searcher of hearts, Thou knowest us better than we know ourselves, and seest the sins which our sinfulness hides from us. Yet even our own conscience beareth witness against us, that we often slumber on our appointed watch; that we walk not always lovingly with each other, and humbly with Thee; and we withhold that entire sacrifice of ourselves to Thy perfect will, without which we are not crucified with Christ or sharers in His redemption. O look upon our contrition, and lift up our weakness, and let the dayspring yet arise within our hearts, and bring us healing, strength and joy. Day by day may we grow in faith, in self-denial, in charity in heavenly-mindedness. And then mingle us at last with the mighty host of Thy redeemed for evermore. Amen." (James Martineau, born 1805)

The World Must Be Shown

One afternoon more than forty years ago I was sitting in a hammock in a little thatched house in eastern Ecuador. On the floor sat Minkayi, an Auca Indian, telling a story into the plastic microphone of a little old-fashioned tape recorder. This is what he was saying:

"One morning I had gone a short distance in my canoe when I heard the knocking of another man's canoe pole. It was Dabu. 'Are you going home?' I asked him. 'Yes,' he said, 'Naenkiwi says those foreigners are cannibals.' Later I found Gikita and Dyuwi putting red dye on their spears, getting them ready. 'Naenkiwi says those foreigners are going to eat us,' they told me. I still had not dyed my spears, but when afternoon came they had all dyed theirs and I was just sitting there. Finally I told my mother to go down and bring my spears up so I could dye them. 'Just bring a few,' I said, and off she went. I asked Naenkiwi how many spears he had. 'Two hard ones and two lightweight ones,' he said."

Minkayi's story ran to six pages. He got pretty excited, telling me how he and five other men had ambushed five white men one afternoon on the Curaray River. He described the journey to the beach, up hills, across rivers, through an old clearing where he had once seen a jaguar, finally reaching the place where a small airplane landed. He said one of these foreigners was walking up and down the beach, calling out, *"Puinani! E ati puinani!"* which means "Come! Come as friends! Come without harm!"

"But we rushed at them with our spears and war cries," Minkayi said, making the vivid sound of spears striking living flesh. He spared none of the details of the long struggle, the suffering, and the Indians' final victory when five white men lay dead.

It seemed impossible to me that this cheerful, friendly man had killed my husband. He picked up Jim Elliot's picture from the top of the kerosene box that served as my bookcase. "Look at him smiling at us!" he said. "If we had known him as we know you, he'd be sitting here, smiling at us today! A cannibal! We thought he was a cannibal!" The absurdity of it struck him funny. A big grin broke over his face.

There was nothing new to Minkayi about killing people. He and others had done it countless times. If you think you are going to be eaten you protect yourself somehow. I thought of Jesus' words when He was about to leave His disciples: "The time is coming when anyone who kills you will suppose he is performing a religious duty. They will do these things because they do not know either the Father or me. I have told you all this so that when the time comes for it to happen you may remember my warning. I have told you this to guard you against the breakdown of your faith."

Jesus did not want his disciples to put their faith in the wrong places. He reminded them in no uncertain terms that things happen—things we don't plan. What kind of certainty, what sort of protection, can we expect if we're realistic? The world talks about "securities." That usually means money in some form or other, and we all know that money insures nobody against anything. What they call life insurance is really death insurance—death and taxes are two things we can count on. You may insure your house and it gets robbed or burned down or the roof blows off or termites chew it to bits. You pay for health insurance and then you get some weird disease that isn't covered. Somebody rear-ends your car and sues you because there was ice on the road.

But what about us Christians? Have we some guarantees? If we really pray hard enough and go to church and read the Bible and all that, don't we have a right to expect that the worst disasters will miss us and things won't be quite so bad for us as they are for everybody else?

Once upon a time some Indians sharpened up their spears and then used them on some Christian men who had hoped to give them the Word of God. Those men knew that death was a possibility. They sang a hymn together: "We rest on Thee, our Shield and our Defender." The territory was dangerous but they went in obedience to Jesus Christ, trusting that He would give them success.

But Aucas know how to throw spears. Could God have prevented those spears from reaching their targets? Yes. Did He? No. Mystery is something we must all come to terms with. "If God were small enough to be understood He would not be big enough to be worshipped" (Evelyn Underhill).

Dr. J.I. Packer says, "The popular idea of faith is of a certain obstinate optimism: the hope, tenaciously held in the face of trouble, that the universe is fundamentally friendly and things may get better." I would have had to be an optimist of the most incorrigible obstinacy to have held onto that sort of faith in the dark times of my own life. It has been the faith of the Son of God who loves me and gave Himself for me that has held me in the darkest valley and the hottest fires and the deepest waters. He too went down to death for our sakes. He too was misunderstood, doubted, hated, and finally nailed to a cross.

Packer says faith requires a going out to, laying hold of, and resting upon the object of its confidence. What we need to see today is that if the object of our confidence is the blueprint we've worked out for ourselves, we're in trouble. If the blueprint doesn't work, the faith doesn't work. If what we call "our faith" means what we think God ought to do about things, it won't last long if He doesn't do it our way.

> Blind unbelief is sure to err and scan His work in vain.
> God is His own interpreter, and He will make it plain.

How do you suppose Daniel felt about having to be dumped into that den of starving lions? What about his friends who were tied up and heaved into a blazing furnace? What about Paul, who was beaten with rods, stoned, shipwrecked, and imprisoned? Well of course the endings of those stories were happy—the lions didn't eat Daniel, the furnace didn't burn up Shadrach, Meshach, and Abednego, and Paul survived—for a while. But then there was John the Baptist who had his head chopped off because he was obeying his Lord and Master. Stephen was stoned to death for preaching the gospel. The book of Hebrews tells about people who were sawn in two because of their faith!

And shall we forget the price our sinless Savior paid for our redemption? He was captured, blindfolded, slapped, punched, whipped, stripped, crowned with thorns, and nailed to a wooden Cross with real iron nails. Think about that.

The real question we need to face is exactly what a Christian is supposed to do when terrible things happen. There are two choices, and only two: We can trust God or we can defy Him. We believe that God is God, He's still got the whole world in His hands and knows exactly what He's doing, or we must believe that He is not God and we are at the awful mercy of mere chance.

Jesus did not promise physical safety for His disciples. He did not expect it for Himself. Just before His death He said, "I shall not talk much longer with you, for the Prince of this world approaches." You know who that was: Satan, of course, coming to gloat over Jesus' capture and betrayal and crucifixion. It was going to happen for sure. Jesus knew it. But listen to what He said next: "He has not rights over me, but the world must be shown that I love the Father and do exactly what he commands."

Satan was given permission for a while. Satan is allowed to do appalling things today too. For a while. Divine permission is given for many frightening things—for a while. But Christians know what the end will be—the kingdoms of this world will become the kingdoms of our Lord and of His Christ and He shall reign forever and ever.

But in the meantime, the world must be shown. There has to be living proof that some men and some women today actually love God and will do exactly what He says. My husband and I have been in India, China, Mongolia, and many other countries. In each country we meet people who, because of the story of five American missionaries killed by the Aucas, have committed themselves unreservedly to Christ.

Faith is a decision. It is not a deduction from the facts around us. We would not look at the world of today and logically conclude that God loves us. It doesn't always look as though He does. Faith is not an instinct. It certainly is not a feeling—feelings don't help much when you're in the lions' den or hanging on a wooden Cross. Faith is not inferred from the happy way things always work. It is an act of the will, a choice, based on the unbreakable Word of a God who cannot lie, and who showed us what love and obedience and sacrifice mean, in the person of Jesus Christ.

So while we live and work, the world must be shown, uncompromisingly, clearly, unapologetically—as Daniel and Paul and five young missionaries and Jesus Himself demonstrated—that we love God and will by His grace obey.

For most of us, it will not mean lions' dens or Auca spears or imprisonment, but it will mean a daily, faithful, humble, glad obedience to the same Lord who has held steady all those who commit themselves to Him. It will mean the choice between faith and unbelief, between being honest on your income tax or cheating just a little bit, between keeping your virginity until marriage or giving it away to somebody you aren't married to. It will mean the willingness to stand against what everybody's doing and what everybody says is OK. It will mean the surrender of what the world calls safety, and the acceptance of whatever sacrifice and suffering God may choose to send. He is not finished with any of us. He assigns me new lessons every day. When I have disobeyed it has led to misery. When I have obeyed it has brought me joy. The story is God's story. The end will be glorious beyond our wildest dreams—for those who put their trust in Him.

Do it! Choose Jesus Christ! Deny yourself, take up the Cross, and follow Him—for the world must be shown. The world must see, in us, a discernible, visible, startling difference.

Put your trust in Him. Not in people or circumstances or dreams or programs or plans, not in any human notion of what will or won't happen, but in the God of Abraham, Isaac, and Jacob, of Daniel and all the others—the God whose Son went through the darkest valleys so that you and I might be saved. If somebody was willing to give his life for you, would you trust him? Of course you would. Jesus loved you then. He loves you now. He'll be loving you every minute of every hour of every day of the rest of your life, and no matter what happens, nothing can separate you from that love. I know it's true. I have found that sure and steadfast Refuge in my Lord and Savior—the only real safety—the Everlasting Arms! I've walked with God a long time. I know He keeps His promises.

Faith for the Unexplained

*W*e know that to those who love God, who are called according to his plan, everything that happens fits into a pattern for good" (Romans 8:28, PHILLIPS). Most of us have heard that verse quoted when we were in the throes of something that did not seem as though it could possibly fit into any such pattern. If the evidence for this astounding statement were perfectly obvious to us right then and there, we should accept the truth without question. There would be no room for doubt. Everything would be explainable, so there would be no room for faith either! We would simply accept the written Word unthinkingly, as a matter of course, without the exercise of intelligence or the discipline of faith, for faith goes to work where there are no explanations.

"I am telling you this now," said Jesus, "so that your faith in me may not be shaken" (John 16:1, PHILLIPS). He knew from his own life experience here on earth that everything else is shakable. He was, of course, perfect God, but He was also perfect *man* having both the nature of God and the nature of man. As man He prayed, He submitted, He obeyed, and "He *learned* obedience from what he *suffered*" (Hebrews 5:8, italics mine).

This is a great mystery and it requires costly faith. It is a necessary part of our Christian life that we should be puzzled by this and even scandalized. "This man was handed over to you by God's set purpose and foreknowledge; and you, with the help of wicked men, put him to death by nailing him to the cross" (Acts 2:23). Here we are face-to-face with that mystery which theologians describe as Will and Necessity—the will of God and the necessity of evil.

Is there a more nettling and problematic passage in the Bible than Acts 2:23—unless it is Acts 4:27 and 28? Whenever we ask, "But how can God allow (this or that)?" our mouths are stopped by this unfathomable paradox.

Ronald Knox writes, "Take the mystery of grace and free will. How, you ask, can one and the same action, at one and the same time, be God's action and mine? It's impossible. But no, you see … free will is a mystery that defies all explanation and when you think you have come across an explanation you find that, after all, you have left the facts out of the account."

When we are stalling over some difficult decision, or hesitating to make an affirmation, *faith* comes in to strengthen and encourage us, but faith's object is dim to your human eyes. In the face of obscurities Jesus is saying, "Trust Me." Grace then is given which confirms our will and helps us toward a faith which can rest with the unexplained.

On Asking Questions

*O*ne often hears people say, "The first question I'm going to ask God when I get to heaven is ..." During His final discourse with the disciples before He went to the cross they were asking Him many questions. Jesus said to them, "Now is your time of grief, but I will see you again and you will rejoice, and no one will take away your joy. In that day you will no longer ask me anything" (John 16:22-23). The King James Version says, "You will ask me no question." May not the sight of Jesus Himself in His glory make all our questions seem redundant, if not simply foolish? I'm sure I will be speechless.

The Parable of the Sower teaches us that often there is not a willing reception of the Word of God. The seed falls on the footpath (e.g., the well-worn, accepted notions of the world) and Satan takes away what has been sown. Some falls on rocks, and has no staying power (when there is trouble we easily give up). Some falls among thistles (the worries of this world, the false glamour of riches, ambitions that choke out the life). And some, Jesus said, falls on good soil. His word is heard, welcomed, and produces fruit.

There are not many new questions in our very human hearts. When I examine my own heart and find that I am tempted to say to the Lord, "Yes, but—" or "What about—?" or "How can I possibly—?" I find that He has questions for me:

Are you willing to understand?
  To rearrange your life?
  To be healed?
  To lose your life for my sake?
Do you want solutions or holiness?
  Answers or orders?
  The light of Christ or your own logic?

And the still small voice says, *You must become like a little child.*

What does this mean? I must ask myself: Do I treat the truth of God as though it were something to be tinkered with or something to be submitted to? Do I ask, "What will this *do*—to my friend or to my plans or to myself?" God tells me I must leave such questions to Him, and do at once the thing He requires. My parents usually treated delayed obedience as disobedience. He who hesitated risked a spanking! How much more quickly we would find the answer we worry about if we just set about doing the thing the Lord tells us to do. Obedience opens our eyes. Do it, with childlike faith, no matter what the cost, for "whoever cares for his own safety is lost; but if a man will let himself be lost for my sake, he will find his true self" (Matthew 16:25, NEB).

Some of your questions, Romano Guardini says, are "afflictions of the heart that have assumed intellectual proportions." Evelyn Underhill puts it this way: "It is only disguised pride that makes us fret over what we can't understand."

God will see to it that we understand as much truth as we are willing to obey. "He who belongs to God hears what God says," Jesus told the Jews who were arguing with Him. "The reason you do not hear is that you do not belong to God" (John 8:47). In other words, one's commitment to God—a total self-abandonment—is prerequisite to hearing. When we wonder how God will do a thing this may spring from spiritual lust: I must have an explanation! We demand an answer when we ought to pray for a deeper confidence in Him who is the Answer. A simple heart, full of love for God, will soon learn what to do. Questions will be quieted. "The fruit of righteousness will be peace; the effect of righteousness will be quietness and confidence forever. My people will live in peaceful dwelling places, in secure homes, in undisturbed places of rest" (Isaiah 32:17-18).

Dear old George MacDonald always has a gentle understanding of our humanness and God's merciful lovingkindness. He writes, "Questions imply answers. If God has put the question in my heart, then He must hold the answer in His. I will seek them from Him. I will wait, but not until I have knocked. I will be patient, but not until I have asked. I will seek until I find. He has something for me. My prayers shall go up unto the God of my life" (*Unspoken Sermons,* First series, "The Higher Faith").

Why Did Jesus Die?

*H*is popularity with the multitudes aroused jealousy in the teachers of the law. There was much muttering. "He is baptizing and everyone is going to him." Some said He was a good man. No, said others, He is leading people astray. How come He speaks with such wisdom when He has never studied? Could this possibly be the Christ? Surely He is not from God—He has a demon. He is mad. He speaks blasphemously.

A meeting of the Sanhedrin was called.

"What are we accomplishing?" they asked. "Here is this man performing many miraculous signs. If we let him go on like this, everyone will believe in him, and then the Romans will come and take away both our place and our nation."

The crowd that had seen Lazarus walk out of the tomb had spread far and wide the word about a miracle worker. This was the last straw. "See," said the Pharisees, "this is getting us nowhere. Look how the whole world has gone after him!"

This man Jesus was not to be tolerated.

That much is not surprising. We understand politics, which certainly had a part in His death. But politics was not the real and inescapable cause. There was something far deeper, unimaginably deeper, which we may spend our lives seeking to fathom. It is revealed in Jesus' words to His disciples at the Last Supper: "This is my body given for you."

For us. For us who desperately need redemption Jesus *gave His* body. No one could have taken His life from Him. He laid it down of his own volition, to redeem us, for we had sinned. In the person of Adam we had made a declaration of independence—to "do our own thing"—and thus had fallen away from God, "in the terrible, literal sense of the word, towards the negative nothingness of sin, destruction, death, senselessness and the abyss," as Romano Guardini describes it. "God's mysterious grace could not leave man in such forlornness; it desired to help him home, in a manner of such sacred magnanimity and power, that once revealed to us, it is impossible to conceive of any other: in the manner of *love*" (abridged from Romano Guardini, *The Lord*).

He wanted to help us home! Why? There are at least sixteen specific expressions of that divine compassion. I list them in the order in which they are found in Scripture:

1. that we might not perish, but have eternal life
2. to justify us
3. to establish His lordship
4. that we might cease to live for ourselves
5. to rescue us out of this present age of wickedness
6. in order that we might attain the status of sons
7. that we might live in company with Him
8. to save sinners
9. to win freedom for all
10. to make us a pure people, marked out for His own
11. that we might cease to live for sin
12. to bring us to God
13. to do away with sin

14. to undo the devil's work
15. to bring us life
16. as the remedy for the defilement of sin

Ezra the prophet, writing four centuries before Christ, knew nothing, of course, of the Cross, but prayed, "Our God, you have punished us less than our sins deserved. Here we are before you in our guilt, though because of it not one of us can stand in your presence." Nor can we. We have a far greater revelation, in the New Testament, of the enormity of our sin, and we know about the Cross. What shall we do about it?

Matthew and Mark tells us that the two criminals who hung on crosses beside Jesus heaped insults on Him at first. One of them said, "Aren't you the Christ? Save yourself and us!" But the other, with new insight, recognizing the justice of his own punishment and the innocence of Jesus, asked to be remembered in the kingdom. "Today," Jesus said, "you will be with Me in Paradise."

How shall we respond to this inconceivable sacrifice of love? In 1949, when Jim Elliot was a senior in college, he wrote:

I set My love upon thee, child,
I knew thee far away.
I wept to see thee wandering wild,
I yearned till thou didst pray.

One of a rebel, hateful band,
Strong in thy lust for sin,
A furtive, fitful, fiery soul—

I loved, I called thee in.

I stripped thee of thy grimy pride,
Laid bare thy secret want—
Poor vagabond of empty ways!
I sent My Spirit to haunt.

Now, desert son, the choice is thine;
My love thou canst forget
And go to roaming wasteland paths.
Wilt, willful, wander yet?

Jesus asks us to take up the cross—to take it up daily. What does this mean? Surely it is the quiet acceptance of disappointments, the willing performance of some hard task we'd prefer to avoid or some small duty which is distasteful to us. It is forgiveness to that one who has deeply wronged us and has not apologized (the Lord tells us to forgive those who *trespass*, not only those who apologize!). The cross is offered to us every day in some form, at times comparatively trivial, at other times real suffering, but it is always something which slashes straight across our human nature, for the cross was an instrument of torture. Paul knew far more about crosses than most of us will ever know. In addition to floggings, imprisonments, and shipwrecks, he mentioned, "When we are cursed, we bless; when we are persecuted, we endure it; when we are slandered, we answer kindly. Up to this moment we have become the scum of the earth."

It was he who said, "I have been crucified with Christ.... The life I live in the body, I live by faith in the Son of God, who loved me and gave himself for me" (Galatians 2:20). We are not only reminded of Him who took up gladly a real cross of real wood and real nails—"a worm, and not a man"—we are also bidden to sing of the Resurrection:

> *He closed the yawning gates of hell*
> *The bars from Heaven's high portals fell;*
> *Let hymns of praise His triumph tell!*
> *Alleluia!*
>
> *Lord! by the stripes which wounded Thee,*
> *From death's dread sting*
> *Thy servant free*
> *That we may live and sing to Thee,*
> *Alleluia!*

(Latin hymn, 1675)

Moses and Mothering

oses heard the people of every family wailing, each at the entrance to his tent. The Lord became exceedingly angry, and Moses was troubled. He asked the Lord,

> Why have you brought this trouble on your servant? What have I done to displease you that you put the burden of all these people on me? Did I conceive all these people? Did I give them birth? Why do you tell me to carry them in my arms, as a nurse carries an infant, to the land you promised on oath to their forefathers? Where can I get meat for all these people? They keep wailing to me, "Give us meat to eat!" I cannot carry all these people by myself; the burden is too heavy for me. If this is how you are going to treat me, put me to death right now.
>
> NUMBERS 11:10-15

Had you thought about Moses having to *mother* the people of Israel? What a job he was given! Any mother realizes that the job is too big for anyone to do alone. Moses would rather die than bear such a burden by himself. But, of course, he did not have to do it alone. The Lord helped him.

Yet Moses suffered. While he was praying and fasting on the mountain, terrible things happened down in the camp. There was a riot. An idolatrous cult had been formed around a golden calf that his own brother had made. In fury he smashed the stone tablets, ground the calf to a powder, and made the people drink it.

Moses, the man responsible before God for his chosen tribe, has been called the most plagued of men. It was struggle from beginning to end. The people would promise obedience, and disobey. They started things and didn't finish. When they met difficulties, they pouted and said that God didn't love them. They forgot His gracious signs and miracles of mercy. The pillar of cloud and fire, the steady sign of the divine presence protecting and guiding them, they ignored. They had no idea of the greatness of their leader. They were blind, unmanageable, "stiffnecked," faithless, lazy. When even God said, "Let me destroy them!" it was Moses who took their part and stood his ground. But the test became so great that his faith failed. He disobeyed in striking the rock when he was told only to speak to it, and for this he was barred from ever entering the Promised Land.

To me, one of the most remarkable proofs of his earnestness in carrying out the charge is his continued obedience, day by day, after he had been told he would never be allowed into Canaan. It was like Job's, "Though he slay me, yet will I trust in him" (Job 13:15, KJV). Moses was saying, "Though He punish me, yet will I obey Him."

Isn't it wonderful that *Moses,* the most plagued of men, was one of the two who appeared on the mountain to Jesus, who was very soon to take up His own bitter Cross for the sake of His people? May all who bear responsibility or authority find strength and encouragement in Moses' endurance and faithfulness.

"Grant unto us, Almighty God, of Thy good Spirit, that quiet heart, and that patient lowliness to which Thy comforting Spirit comes; that we, being humble toward Thee, and loving toward one another, may have our hearts prepared for that peace of Thine which passeth understanding; which if we have, the storms of life can hurt us but little, and the cares of life vex us not at all; in presence of which death shall lose its sting, and the grave its terror; and we, in calm joy, walk all the days our appointed time, until our great change shall come. Amen." (George Dawson, 1821-1876)

FOUR

❧

FINDING CONTENTMENT

The Gift of Place

It is always possible to do the will of God. In every place and time it is within our power to acquiesce in the will of God. Jesus comforted His disciples: "Do not let your hearts be troubled. Trust in God, trust also in me. In my Father's house are many rooms; if it were not so, I would have told you. I am going there to prepare a place for you" (John 14:1-2). Who is finally responsible for our circumstances? Psalm 16:5 tells us: "Lord, you have assigned me my portion and my cup; you have made my lot secure."

We have the assurance—a calming and quieting one—that God in His infinite wisdom has placed us where we are. There are perhaps some factors which we would not happily have chosen.

When Alexander Solzhenitsyn was in prison he wrote, "How simple for me to live with You, O Lord! How easy to believe in You! When in confusion my soul bares itself or bends, when the most wise can see no further than this night and do not know what tomorrow brings, You fill me with the clear certainty that You exist, and that You watch to see that all the paths of righteousness be not closed. From the heights of worldly glory I am astonished by the path through despair you have provided me, this path from which I have been worthy enough to reflect Your radiance to men. All that I will yet reflect You will grant me. And for that which I will not succeed in reflecting, You have appointed others."

Let us never suppose that obedience is impossible or that holiness is meant only for a select few. Our Shepherd leads us in paths of righteousness—not for *our* name's sake but for His. He saw to it that in the midst of excruciating suffering those paths were not closed to Solzhenitsyn. They are not closed to us.

All of us, I suppose, have at times felt strangely displaced, wondering how on earth we landed in a situation so far removed from that of our choosing. In 1958, I was living with Auca Indians in the Ecuadorian jungle. They had provided Valerie and me with a house—"a gift of place," bless their dear hearts! It was identical to their own houses—without walls, floor or furniture. My hammock was swung, as theirs were, between two of the six poles that held up the roof. Valerie, who was three, slept happily in a blanket on split bamboo. Often in the intervals between sleeping and fanning the fire I found myself musing in the wee hours: What am I doing here? How am I to glorify the Lord in such a place? I remembered Psalm 16:5, "Lord, you have assigned me my portion and my cup; you have made my lot secure." I realized that He was preparing *me for* what He was preparing *for me*. "I go to prepare a place for you," He told His disciples.

Our heavenly Father knows to place us where we may learn lessons impossible anywhere else. He has neither misplaced nor displaced us. He assigns and designs according to His inscrutable wisdom—always for our blessing and conformity to the image of Christ.

The apostle Paul learned "to be content whatever the circumstances. I know what it is to be in need, and I know what it is to have plenty. I have learned the secret of being content in any and every situation, whether well fed or hungry, whether living in plenty or in want. I can do everything through him who gives me strength" (Philippians 4:11-13).

I believe that in every time and place it is within our power to acquiesce in the will of God—and what peace it brings to do so!

"O Lord, whose way is perfect, help us, I pray Thee, always to trust in Thy goodness: that walking with Thee and following Thee in all simplicity, we may possess quiet and contented minds; and may cast all our care on Thee, for Thou carest for us. Amen." (Christina Rosetti)

Garage Sales

Garage sales are a great way to unload everything you aren't using anymore. I'm all for people *having* sales, but I'm not much of a customer, though I once spent five dollars on an electric mixer and fifty for a recliner for my son-in-law. As I survey what's for sale I wonder what it tells us about American life.

Restlessness. Discontent. Ceaseless activity. Short attention span.

The skis and skates and surfboards have perhaps been outgrown by the children. That's understandable. But the Ski-Doos and scuba-diving stuff, all those cute and clever but unnecessary gadgets, the expensive exercise machines, the tables loaded with useless bric-a-brac—I suspect it was adults who thought they needed those.

A life lived without reflection can be very superficial and empty. The emptiness must be filled. Not knowing the One who alone can fill the heart, man grabs repeatedly for some new stimulation, sensation, satisfaction to fill his time and slake his restlessness. His enjoyment is short-lived. What he got for Christmas or bought at a garage sale last year he soon tires of. It furnishes him with goods for his own garage sale. He is like the man who wrote, "I denied myself nothing my eyes desired; I refused my heart no pleasure.... Yet when I surveyed all that my hands had done and what I had toiled to achieve, everything was meaningless, a chasing after the wind" (Ecclesiastes 2:10-11).

How much is enough? "Godliness with contentment is great gain" (1 Timothy 6:6).

The more complicated life becomes, the more we need to quiet our souls before God. It is my prayer that the following simple (but not by any means easy) principles may be of help to many, as they have been and continue to be to me. "The Lord God will help me; therefore shall I not be confounded; therefore have I set my face like a flint, and I know that I shall not be ashamed" (Isaiah 50:7, KJV).

1. *Go to God first.* Kneel in silence. Lift up your heart and hands. Listen. "I am ready; let him do to me whatever seems good to him" (2 Samuel 15:26).

2. *Receive the Givens and the Not-Givens.* "Lord, you have assigned me my portion and my cup; you have made my lot secure" (Psalm 16:5).

3. *In acceptance lies peace.* "Peace I leave with you; my peace I give you. I do not give to you as the world gives. Do not let your hearts be troubled and do not be afraid" (John 14:27).

4. *It is always possible to do the will of God.* "If you love me, you will obey what I command" (John 14:15; 15:10).

5. *Do it now.* "I will hasten and not delay to obey your commands" (Psalm 119:60). "You do not even know what will happen tomorrow" (James 4:14).

6. *Love means sacrifice.* "This is how we know what love is: Jesus Christ laid down his life for us. And we ought to lay down our lives for our brothers" (1 John 3:16). See also 1 Corinthians 13:1-8.

7. *Choose your attitude.* "Your attitude should be the same as that of Christ Jesus, who ... made himself nothing, taking the very nature of a servant ... He humbled himself" (Philippians 2:5, 7-8).

8. *Analyze your struggle.* Is it merely delayed obedience? "I run in the path of your commands, for you have set my heart free" (Psalm 119:32).

9. *Give it all to Jesus.* "Whoever wants to save his life will lose it, but whoever loses his life for me will find it" (Matthew 16:25).

10. *Do the next thing.* "In the evening my wife died. The next morning I did as I had been commanded" (Ezekiel 24:18).

11. *Give thanks every day and for everything* (Ephesians 5:20, NEB). "Let a righteous man strike me—it is a kindness; let him rebuke me—it is oil on my head. My head will not refuse it" (Psalm 141:5).

How Much Is Enough?

Speaking of Israel's watchmen God says, "They are dogs with mighty appetites; they never have enough. They are shepherds who lack understanding; they all turn to their own way, each seeks his own gain. 'Come,' each one cries, 'Let me get wine! Let us drink our fill of beer! And tomorrow will be like today, or even far better'" (Isaiah 56:11-12).

How much is enough? Feasting is by no means forbidden in Scripture. Rather, we are enjoined to rejoice and be glad. Have not we that know Jesus Christ great cause for celebrating?

My husband and I were invited, along with six or eight others, to the home of a very wealthy lady in Texas. The menu? A large and delicious salad. Nothing else, as I recall, except perhaps coffee. An unforgettable meal and an unforgettable lesson—it was enough.

Here in America most of us have far, far *more* than enough. Some families have agreed together to scale down gift-giving at Christmas time in order to be more generous to those who are in real need. The proliferation of garage sales indicates that people do eventually come to the realization that they have Too Much Stuff. They put it out for sale and along come folks who, although they are very likely in need of nothing, find something irresistible. They lug it home—but do they set about dealing with what they can now get rid of?

Hudson Taylor, a missionary to China, took stock each year

of all his possessions. Anything which he had not used for a year he felt duty-bound to give to someone who could make good use of it. If you haven't used it for a year, you don't need it! How many suits or dresses does a man or woman really need? Have you counted up the T-shirts or shoes you haven't worn for more than a year? The pens that clutter the back of that drawer? The tapes and CDs you never listen to? The stuff in the hall closet, the basement, or the trunk of the car?

It took Lars and me a few years to wake up to the fact that we could travel much more lightly than most of the people we see in airports. Why, we asked, does anyone want to be burdened with so much stuff? It's enough to make you want to stay at home! What, I wonder, would be my response if the Lord Jesus said to me what He said to those He sent out to the harvest field: "Do not take a purse or bag or sandals"?

As faithful stewards of what we have, ought we not to give earnest thought to our staggering surplus? Remember God's words, "If there is a poor man among your brothers ... do not be hardhearted or tightfisted toward your poor brother" (Deuteronomy 15:7). The word *steward* is an interesting one, derived from the word, *sty,* a pen for pigs, and *ward,* one who guards. First Peter 4:10 reminds us that "each one should use whatever gift he has received to serve others, faithfully administering God's grace in its various forms" (NIV) "as good stewards of the manifold grace of God" (KJV).

A Holy Aloneness

hen God had completed the prodigious labor of the creation of the heavens and the earth, He saw that something was lacking: there was no one to work the ground. So He formed man. The method is surprising—this creature, made in the image of God, was made out of *dust*, and into his nostrils God breathed the breath of life. This living being was placed in a beautiful garden with a river to water it, and gold, aromatic resin, and onyx to enrich it. He put the man there to work the garden and take care of it. I wonder, as Adam went about his task, how conscious he was of the presence of God. Did he walk and talk with Him (in what language?), commune silently or aloud, listen to His voice? Was he aware at all that anything was lacking? God was aware. "It is not good for the man to be alone," said God. "I will make a helper suitable for him." Eve was created, God's gift to allay Adam's loneliness. But when he capitulated to her ungodly counsel, sin was born.

The world is full of noise. As Wordsworth said, "Late and soon, getting and spending, we lay waste our powers." Might we not set ourselves to learn silence, stillness, solitude? It will not be easy to come by. It must be arranged. The Lord Jesus, available to people much of the time, left them, sometimes a great while before day, to go up to the hills where He could commune in solitude with His Father. Job, enduring his friends' tiresome lectures and accusations, was very much alone on his ash heap, but it was there that he came to know God as never before. When Paul received God's call to preach the gospel he did not consult anyone. He went into Arabia. The old apostle John, when exiled to Patmos, must surely have known a *holy aloneness* through which he received the book of Revelation.

Someone may complain that he has no one to talk to. Then thank God! Talk to Him. When my husband Jim Elliot died in Ecuador I was blessed to have my ten-month-old baby and many dear Quichua friends, but we lived deep in the jungle and I longed at times for in-depth conversation in my own language. The Quichuas were very solicitous—they had loved Jim as their pastor, teacher, and friend. All of us were bereaved, but it was my job to be cheerful and try to strengthen and encourage the Indians, who had very little Scripture as yet in their own language and were accustomed to heathen howling when someone died.

We can always talk to God, remembering that God has called us into fellowship with Jesus Christ our Lord (1 Corinthians 1:9). Do we consciously arrange time to receive His fellowship? When is the last time we offered Him ours? It is a strong temptation to run to the phone when we need advice or help of any kind, forgetting to seek *first* the living Word of God, whose ear is always open to our cry. Try the simple reminder of 2 Peter 2:9, "The Lord knows how to rescue godly men from trials," or Psalm 57:1, "Have mercy on me, O God, have mercy on me, for in you my soul takes refuge. I will take refuge in the shadow of your wings until disaster has passed."

Be patient. Is God not fast enough? Are His answers too

tough? A quick sympathy from a friend may suggest that you simply drop out, be good to yourself, get away from it all. Someone else will be sure to say, "You need counsel." Are you sure? One hour at the foot of the Cross may obviate the necessity of professional counseling (no such thing existed until the twentieth century—what did folks do before then?). When Christian, in *Pilgrim's Progress,* reached the hill of Calvary, "his burden loosed from off his shoulders, and fell from off his back, and began to tumble; and so continued to do, till it came to the mouth of the Sepulchre, where it fell in." The Bible teaches us that here is a Wonderful Counselor. Let your loneliness be transformed into a holy aloneness. Sit still before the Lord. Remember Naomi's word to Ruth: "Sit still, my daughter, until you see how the matter will fall."

Miguel de Molinos (1640-97) wrote, "In times of trouble go not out of yourself to seek for aid; for the whole benefit of trial consists in silence, patience, rest, and resignation. In this condition divine strength is found for the hard warfare, because God Himself fights for the soul."

A Hard Decision

*W*hen Moses, that sorely tried man, was approached by the daughter of Zelophehad (in Numbers 27) I wonder if he was tempted to say to himself, "*Now* what do these women want?" It was a hard case. Their father had died (because of his own sins), he had left no son, and the women wanted property among his relatives in order that his name not disappear from the clan.

When faced with hard decisions, do what Moses did. "Moses brought their case before the Lord." What a difference it makes when one lays the difficulty immediately before God. God answers.

When there is perplexity there is always guidance—not always at the moment we ask, but in good time, which is God's time. There is no need to fret and stew.

This was the last decision Moses had to make before God's revelation to him of his own and his brother Aaron's death. Did he breathe a sigh of relief that his responsibility was finished? Did he flinch at the realization that his life was over? There was no complaint, only the question as to who would take the leadership of the flock. (Sometimes we worry about decisions which are not ours to make.) Moses knew where to take that concern.

"May the Lord, the God of the spirits of all mankind, appoint a man over this community to go out and come in before them, one who will lead them out and bring them in, so the Lord's people will not be like sheep without a shepherd." In spite of all the trial those people had put him through, Moses never said, "I've *had* it." He continued to shepherd them, carrying them on his heart for God's very best.

Decision-making always puts our faith on trial. Is our life our own or does it belong to Another? Will the Lord show us the way? Will we follow where He leads? Are we meek enough to be instructed? We are told that Moses—a powerful leader, God's choice to deliver Israel—was the meekest of men. But he had had long years of training—in the care of sheep and goats!—the best training, no doubt, for dealing with a rebellious people.

Yet at the end of his life he faced perhaps the hardest discipline ever required of him. He was not to be allowed to enter the Promised Land because he had dishonored God before the people. When told to speak to the rock he had struck it in anger and impatience. For that he was barred from the fulfillment of his cherished dream to reach Canaan, to which he had long looked forward.

Moses was now redundant—a blow that crushed many a man—but he accepted this meekly and quietly. What a lesson for all of us.

When faced with a hard decision, go to God first of all. When assigned a hard discipline, accept it.

"Do thy first duty," said Thomas Carlyle. "The second will become clear."

The Sufferings of a Housewife

A young mother asked how on earth she is to learn to love the Lord, grow in grace, and be truly holy in the midst of general chaos—hard work, very limited means, little chance for fellowship, and her own children disobeying, screaming, and fighting.

It is tempting to imagine that, given a different lot in life, circumstances other than those in which we find ourselves, we would make much greater strides in holiness. The truth is that the place where we *are* is God's schoolroom, not somewhere else. *Here* we may be conformed to the likeness of Christ.

It takes adversity of one kind or another. There is no other way. "It has been granted to you on behalf of Christ not only to believe on him but also to suffer for him" (Philippians 1:29). This dear woman had not thought of the word "suffering." To her it was just the awful "dailyness of husband and children, the same dishes and clothes to be washed, the house to be cleaned a thousand times, the monotonous repetition of "Do this," "Don't do that," the sheer unmanageability of it all.

"God is asking you simply to be what you are," I told the young mother, and to be just that with love, with her heart's acceptance, and without fretting. How comforting to know that the Lord who made us never forgets that we are *dust!* Our love will fail, our heart will balk, we will fret. But our very powerlessness is the place where *His* power is manifested, where His all-sufficient grace is given.

The trivial round, the common task,
Will furnish all we ought to ask—
Room to deny ourselves, a road
To bring us daily nearer to God.

(John Keble, 1822)

Hannah Whitall Smith said, "He does not need to transplant us into a different field.... He transforms the very things that were before our greatest hindrances, into the chiefest and most blessed means of our growth. No difficulties in your case can baffle Him.... Put yourself absolutely into His hands, and let Him have His own way with you."

To Offer Thanks

*L*etters come to me from childless women who long for children—and from women who are terribly upset to find themselves pregnant again. God is the Lord of life and He gives His children what is good. It is not always easy to receive thankfully what He apportions.

One correspondent, who had had four children in four and half years, morning sickness every day, a husband who continued to pursue his boat-racing, bowling, fishing, hunting, and golfing, felt she could not cope. There was never enough money. "Had abortions been as readily available then as they are now, I am sure I would have considered it even though I knew it was wrong," she said. But she had a mother whose faithful prayers, emotional support, and practical help enabled her to get through those years.

"Let me tell you, thirty-one years later, how the Lord has blessed us, not because of anything special that we have done, but because He is faithful. Not once have we had the heartache of a wayward child. All are Christians with Christian spouses, all active in their churches. We recently celebrated Christmas together, including eleven grandchildren. I can't tell you the joy we have as a family. I want to encourage young mothers to remember the Lord is in control. Sure, they will be very busy, but the years go by quickly and the rewards are tremendous. Put your trust in the Lord—He will bless you for it!"

One who is yet childless after many prayers for fertility writes that she found herself pulling away from the young married people at church. But having read of a young widow's hope that God still had a plan for *her*, this would-be mother began to thank God for all the blessings He had given instead of dwelling on what He had withheld. "I still desire to have a child, but am also allowing my heavenly Father to work His own desires through my life."

Another writes, "We discovered this past fall that our third child will arrive in June. We had not closed the door to more children but the timing of this one was definitely not in our plans. The news shocked and numbed me for a few days, but I now sense a new awareness of God's sovereignty in our lives—an overruling of our plans for His, and there is tremendous peace in that. When we announced our expectancy at a family get-together one would have thought we had just announced a *divorce*. It's upsetting to see how our society's anti-child, zero-population-growth propaganda has crept into the church.

"My wonderful husband's response to the outcome of the pregnancy test was, "Well, we did what we could to prevent it but God just insists on blessing us!"'

Thanksgiving brings contentment.

Many people seem to be looking ceaselessly for amusement, for some alleviation from boredom. Dissatisfied and restless, they fritter away their lives, wishing to move from what or where they are to what or where they aren't.

"My people have committed two sins," says the Lord in Jeremiah 2:13. "They have forsaken me, the spring of living water, and have dug their own cisterns, broken cisterns that cannot hold water."

Discontent dries up the soul.

I hope you know more than one person to whom you could point and say, "*There* is a truly contented person." Such a one will have learned the lesson of the psalmist, "My heart is not proud, O Lord, my eyes are not haughty; I do not concern myself with great matters or things too wonderful for me" (Psalm 131:1-2) There will be in that man or woman a noticeable peace, "the kind of peace that only I can give," said Jesus. "It is not like the peace that this world can give. So don't be worried or afraid" (John 14:27, CEV).

To love God is to *love His will.* It is to wait quietly for life to be measured out by One who knows us through and through. It is to be content with His timing and His wise apportionment (Do I feel that my portion is too much of something? Too little of something else?). It is to follow in the steps of the Master, as did Paul, who was able to say that he had learned contentment no matter what the circumstances. His circumstances when he wrote that? *Prison!* No easy lesson, but "great gain," which is the sum of godliness plus contentment (see 1 Timothy 6:6).

Jesus loved the will of His Father. He embraced the limitations, the necessities, the conditions, the very *chains* of his humanity as he walked and worked here on earth, fulfilling moment by moment His divine commission and the stern demands of His incarnation. Never was there a word or even a look of complaint.

E.B. Pusey (1800-1882) suggested rules for those who wish to gain contentment that surely reflect Jesus' own attitude:

1. Allow thyself to complain of nothing, not even the weather.
2. Never picture thyself to thyself under any circumstances in which thou are not.
3. Never compare thine own lot with that of another.
4. Never allow thyself to dwell on the wish that this or that had been, or were, otherwise than it was, or is. God Almighty loves thee better and more wisely than thou doest thyself.
5. Never dwell on the morrow. Remember that it is God's not thine. The heaviest part of sorrow often is to look forward to it. "The Lord will provide."

"O God, who makest cheerfulness and companion of strength, but apt to take wings in time of sorrow, we humbly beseech Thee that if, in Thy sovereign wisdom, Thou sendest weakness, yet for Thy mercy's sake deny us not the comfort of patience. Lay not more upon us, O heavenly Father, than Thou wilt enable us to bear; and since the fretfulness of our spirits is more hurtful than the heaviness of our burden, grant us that heavenly calmness which comes of owning Thy hand in all things, and patience in the trust that Thou doest all things well. Amen." (Rowland Williams, 1818-1870)

Summertime in Strawberry Cove

"The lines have fallen unto me in pleasant places," wrote the psalmist, and my gratitude echoes his words. Strawberry Cove is a cul de sac with seven houses, just off Hesperus Avenue in the little town of Magnolia (too small to be on the map), in Massachusetts. You may remember Longfellow's poem, "The Wreck of the Hesperus," the story of the schooner Hesperus, that "sailed the wintry sea," and was wrecked on the rock named Norman's Woe, lying beyond my vision to the east as I sit at my desk.

I look down a grassy bank, humpy with the ceaseless industry of countless woodchucks over countless years. They dig a vast labyrinth of tunnels, piling huge mounds of earth on the bank. I enjoy watching them—obese furry brown creatures with blunt snouts, short tails, and short legs with powerful digging forepaws. They waddle or scurry or lazily sun themselves. They used to be my friends. I thought they were awfully cute until they began neatly nipping off *every single* petunia in our teensy garden. Some of the charm now seems to have perished.

At the bottom of the bank are great sheets of rock and a jumble of awesome red-brown boulders surrounding a lovely little tide pool, so crystal clear that I can see straight to its dark red and bright green floor. Once I spotted an Atlantic salmon that had gotten himself marooned there when the tide ebbed.

Our house, which faces due south from Cape Ann, sits about

sixty feet above a wide expanse of what I call ocean (it has waves and swells and seagulls and seagoing vessels of all sizes) but is more accurately named Massachusetts Bay. It glitters and flashes in the sunlight. A billion diamonds dance. The lobster buoys swing and dip on the swells, and on summer weekends we see the little red flags which mark the presence of scuba divers beneath. Early in the morning we hear the soft thub-thub of the lobster boats as they slip into the Cove. We watch the lobster men pull their "pots" (traps), remove the catch, and fling the rotten bait to the wheeling flocks of screaming gulls who always trail them.

The ocean tempers the climate in both winter and summer. It is ten degrees warmer in winter and cooler in the summer than in Hamilton, where we used to live, twelve miles inland. So we seldom have more than a dozen or so really *hot* days. On one or two of these I may venture down to the rocks with my snorkel. It must be high tide and fairly calm, otherwise one is flung against wicked barnacles, making it hazardous either to get in or out of the water.

The water is bone-chilling, but oh, what exquisite mysteries I discover as I put my goggled face into the water! I am instantly in a different world, a magic one, a silent one, and I forget the ice water and gaze at the swaying forests of seaweed, the sunlit colors of starfish and rock, the shining silver of an occasional fish. It is not to be compared, of course, with the Great Barrier Reef where I once snorkeled. The cold North Atlantic is not a tropical paradise, but it holds more beauty than one can fully bear.

We have a picture window in the living room. Over it is a wooden motto, made for me by one of Amy Carmichael's "babies," an old lady who spent her days there in Dohnavur, India, beautifully lettering Scripture texts. This one has Psalm 95:5 (KJV), "The sea is his, and he made it," a simple and completely staggering statement.

God made it. He dried it up with a rebuke. He rolled it back. He spoke to it and the waves calmed. He stirs it up like a pot of ointment (Job 41:31). He causes it to teem with creatures beyond number (Psalm 104:25). He confounded Job with questions such as,

> Who shut up the sea behind doors when it burst forth
>   from the womb,
>   when I made the clouds its garment and wrapped it in
>   thick darkness,
>   when I fixed limits for it and set its doors and bars in
>   place, when I said,
> "This far you may come and no farther; here is where
>   your proud waves halt"?
> Have you journeyed to the springs of the sea or walked
>   in the recesses of the deep?
>
> JOB 38:8-11, 16

Our Lord Jesus loved the sea. He sat by it and taught the people beside it. He once cooked breakfast on the shore. To me it is a daily gift, a joy, a ceaseless reminder of the majesty and beauty of my Heavenly Father.

What Does it Mean to Be Holy?

W hen God finished the work of creation He blessed the seventh day and made it holy. When Moses saw the burning bush in the desert he found that he was standing on holy ground. God's Word tells us that we must be holy because He is holy. Is so awesome a mandate as holiness attainable for us sinners? Hear what the hymn writer T. Binney wrote:

> Oh, how shall I whose native sphere is dark, whose
>   mind is dim,
> Before the Ineffable appear, and on my naked spirit
> ⁓ bear the uncreated beam?

Jesus, who is "the radiance of God's glory and the exact representation of his being" (Hebrews 1:3), shows us the answer to that question, and the way of obedience. He said, "Here I am— It is written about me in the scroll—I have come to do your will, O God" (Hebrews 10:7).

Holiness is not an impossibility for any of us. It means first of all to be set apart, as the vessels in the tabernacle were set apart (consecrated) from ordinary vessels. For us to be holy means the will to do God's will. It means sacrifice—the offering up of my own will (which sometimes seems to me an impossibility) and the acceptance of His. He asks of us nothing which He Himself was unwilling to do. "He had to be made like his brothers in every way, in order that he might become a merciful and faithful high priest in service to God, and that he might make atonement for the sins of the people. Because he himself suffered when he was tempted, he is able to help those who are being tempted" (Hebrews 2:17-18).

There is a way for man to rise to that sublime abode; an offering and a sacrifice, a Holy Spirit's energies, an Advocate with God.

That Advocate is Jesus Christ, who "although he was a son,... learned obedience from what he suffered and, once made perfect, he became the source of eternal salvation for all who obey him" (Hebrews 5:8-9).

These, these prepare us for the sight of holiness above; the sons of ignorance and night may dwell in the eternal Light, through the Eternal Love.

The Lord loves us, and "takes delight in his people; he crowns the humble with salvation" (Psalm 149:4).

There is an *active* practice of holiness as we carry out, for the glory of God, the ordinary duties of each day, faithfully fulfilling the responsibilities given us. The *passive* practice consists in loving acceptance of the unexpected, be it welcome or unwelcome, remembering that we have a wise and sovereign Lord who works in mysterious ways and is never taken by surprise. I heard a comforting word at the Urbana Missionary Convention some years ago. Eric Alexander, a dear Scottish preacher, reminded us that "God is not *worrried* (roll those Rs!) about *anything!*"

Which of these two requirements of holiness (active or passive) is beyond our strength? Remember the words of the apostle Paul: "I have learned the secret of being content in any and every situation.... I can do everything through him who gives me strength" (Philippians 4:12-13). This is all that God demands of us in His work of sanctification. He demands it from the high and the low, from the strong and the weak; in a word, from all, always and everywhere. A promise to which I have clung for many years is the prophetic word in Isaiah 50:7 (KJV), "The Lord God will help me; therefore shall I not be confounded; therefore have I set my face like a flint, and I know that I shall not be ashamed."

Perfection does not consist in *understanding* God's designs but in *submitting* to them, for "we know that in all things God works for the good of those who love him, who have been called according to His purpose" (Romans 8:28). Sometimes the explanation of his purpose (Romans 8:29) is overlooked: "For those God foreknew he also predestined to be conformed to the likeness of his Son." God works in the soul to make it holy—to make it, finally, like Himself. The whole essence of the spiritual life consists in recognizing the designs of God for us at the present moment.

The Vice of Self-Esteem

Letters sometimes come to me from people who are "working on" their self-esteem. Usually they are doing their best to feel good about themselves. It is an exercise in futility.

I read about tests that were given to American and Korean students. The Koreans scored far higher academically than the Americans, but when asked to grade their self-esteem were bewildered by the questions. The Americans on the other hand, well-versed from kindergarten, gave themselves high marks in self-esteem but did poorly academically. We might say they "felt *good*" about "doing *bad*."

Jesus warns us not to seek the approval of men. Must we rise in the world, be "upwardly mobile," aim at fulfillment, self-satisfaction, distinction? Remember the word in 1 John 2:17 (Phillips): "The world and all its passionate desires will one day disappear. But the man who is following God's will is part of the permanent and cannot die."

Amy Carmichael, when offered a royal reward for her service in India, graciously declined. She could not bear the thought of being honored in ways which her Lord Jesus avoided. If one truly wants to be His disciple he must first *give up his right to himself* (a total abandonment), *take up the Cross* (which must mean, sooner or later and in many forms, suffering), and finally *follow*—a daily obedience.

Gerald Vann speaks of "the disease of self-culture." To have peace one must forget himself. To forget himself one must walk in truth. To walk in truth one must love God and his neighbor. When self-esteem is high, self-knowledge is very small.

Oswald Chambers wrote, "If we ever get a glimpse of what we are in the sight of God we will never say, 'Oh I am so unworthy,' because we shall know we are, beyond the possibility of stating it."

Self-esteem leads to rash judgments of others, as in the case of the Pharisee who "stood up and prayed about himself: 'God I thank you that I am not like other men—robbers, evildoers, adulterers—or even this tax collector. I fast twice a week and give a tenth of all I get.'" Jesus made it clear that the man who was justified before God was the one who had acknowledged himself a sinner. (Lord, have mercy upon us!)

"We do not dare to classify or compare ourselves with some who commend themselves. When they measure themselves by themselves and compare themselves with themselves, they are not wise." (2 Corinthians 10:12).

In the process of trying to convince ourselves that we are worthy, we may notice that some people whom we thought unworthy appear now actually to be better than we. This unsettling observation tempts us then to investigate further. The Tempter will gladly cooperate, impressing on our minds others' small failings which we are happy to magnify. Thus we justify ourselves and build our self-esteem. We begin, like the publican, to thank God we are not like those others. But when were we given the office of judge? An examination of our own hearts before God will show us more and more plainly how much work we have to do in ourselves. Little time will be left to pay much attention to the defects of others.

While I disparage the exercise of "building one's self-esteem" I indulge in it every time I imagine myself free from the defects I perceive in someone else. I am, in effect, thanking God that I am not like him or her. "O wretched [woman] that I am! who shall deliver me from the body of this death?" (Romans 7:24, KJV).

We have an adversary called the Devil. He's a malicious serpent, bent on destroying us, and he has quite a bag of tricks, beginning, of course, in the Garden of Eden when he convinced Eve that God meant to deprive her of the one thing she was determined to have. He whispered a delectable thought: *Hath God said?*, thus persuading the woman that obedience was not required. She could have what she chose, and be the better for it. Thus the ruinous and all-pervasive sin of pride was born.

"To preserve thyself from this danger, choose for thy battlefield the safe and level ground of a true and deep conviction of thy own nothingness," wrote Lorenzo Scupoli. Think about the time before we were born. Throughout all that abyss of eternity we were nothing and could have done nothing whatever to bring ourselves into existence. Consider next that we received our being solely because God willed it and sustains us every moment of our lives. Of ourselves we are nothing. "What good or meritorious deed could thy nature perform by itself if deprived of divine assistance?"

J.I. Packer, in *Rediscovering Holiness,* says, "Sin is an … allergic reaction to God's law, an irrational anti-God syndrome that drives us to exalt ourselves and steels our heart against devotion and obedience to our Maker."

And another word from C.S. Lewis:

"The more we get what we call 'ourselves' out of the way and let Him take over, the more truly ourselves we become. In that sense our real selves are all waiting for us in Him….

"But there must be a real giving up of the self. You must throw it away 'blindly' so to speak. Christ will indeed give you a real personality: but you must not go to Him for the sake of that. As long as your own personality is what you are bothering about, you are not going to Him at all. The very first step is to try to forget about self altogether. Lose your life and you will save it. Submit to death, death of your ambitions and favorite wishes every day and death of your body—in the end submit with every fibre of your being, and you will find eternal life. Keep back nothing. Nothing in you that has not died will ever be raised from the dead. Look for yourself, and you will find in the long run only hatred, loneliness, despair, rage, ruin and decay. But look for Christ and you will find Him and with Him everything else thrown in." (From *Beyond Personality*)

"Lord, I do not know what to ask. You alone know what I need. You love me better than I know how to love myself. O Father! Give to your child what she herself is too ignorant to pray for. I dare not ask either for crosses or consolations. I simply present myself before You. I open my heart to You. I adore Your purposes even though I don't know them. I am silent. I offer myself in sacrifice, I yield myself to You. I want to have no other desire than to accomplish Your will. Teach me to pray. Pray You Yourself in me. Amen." (François de la Mothe Fénelon [modern English translation by E.E.])

FIVE

❧

JOY AND SORROW

Joy

Among the most joyful people I have known have been some who seem to have had no human reason for joy. The sweet fragrance of Christ has shown through their lives. I have often spoken about dear old Mrs. Kershaw, a destitute widow who, somehow or other, began to work for my mother. She lived in a bleak old house, sparsely furnished, cold in winter and hot in summer. She had only one son. He rarely visited her. She was in her seventies, poor, humpbacked, and stone deaf. One of us would pick her up in the car each morning. On the door we would find a notice: "I AM HOME. COME IN." She was always sitting in her little rocking chair, black coat and hat on, black bag in her lap. She would look up with a seraphic smile: "Oh, it's the daughter!" she would say if it happened to be my turn to transport her. When she entered our home she had one thing on her mind: *How can I make the Howards happy?* She would set to work—washing dishes, doing laundry, making applesauce or brown sugar cookies, going upstairs to sit with our old, sad, deaf step-grandmother (can you imagine the exchanges in conversation?), and praying for our family. I've never seen a sweeter face and have never met anyone who could have surpassed her in lovingkindness and total self-forgetfulness.

"In that day shall the deaf hear the words of the book.... The meek also shall increase their joy in the Lord, and the poor among men shall rejoice in the Holy One of Israel" (Isaiah 29:18-19, KJV).

"Though you have not seen him, you love him; and even though you do not see him now, you believe in him and are filled with an inexpressible and glorious joy" (1 Peter 1:8).

C.S. Lewis wrote, "Joy is the serious business of heaven." I think Mrs. Kershaw lived in heaven on earth!

Moods

My daughter Valerie Shepard, on one of those days when she felt particularly inadequate as the mother of eight (four were still homeschooled), found help in these wise words from Oswald Chambers:

There are certain things we must not pray about—moods, for instance. Moods never go by praying, moods go by kicking. A mood nearly always has its set in the physical condition, not in the moral. It is a continual effort not to listen to the moods which arise from a physical condition, never submit to them for a second. We have to take ourselves by the scruff of the neck and shake ourselves, and we will find that we can do what we said we would not. The curse with most of us is that we won't. The Christian life is one of incarnate spiritual pluck.

(My Utmost for His Highest)

"Lord! When I am in sorrow, I think on Thee. Listen to the cry of my heart, and my sorrowful complaint. Yet, O Father, I would not prescribe to Thee when and how Thy help should come. I will willingly tarry for the hour which Thou thyself has appointed for my relief. Meanwhile strengthen me by Thy Holy Spirit; strengthen my faith, my hope, my trust; give me patience and resolution to bear my trouble; and let me at last behold the time when Thou wilt make me

glad with Thy grace. Ah, my Father! Never yet hast Thou forsaken Thy children, forsake not me. Ever dost Thou give gladness unto the sorrowful, O give it now unto me. Always dost Thou relieve the wretched, relieve me too, when and where and how Thou wilt. Unto Thy wisdom, love, and goodness, I leave it utterly. Amen." (J.F. Starck, 1680-1756)

Suffering and Joy

In 1976, I learned that Corrie ten Boom was to speak at nearby Gordon College in Wenham, Massachusetts. "Oh!" thought I, "I do hope she will tell us of her prison experience!" Of course, I bought tickets for my daughter and me, and it was with great anticipation that we went. She did indeed tell her story and then, to my astonishment, she invited Valerie and me to have tea with her later that week. When we arrived at the house where she was staying her secretary met us at the door, explained that Corrie was in bed—not ill, just her one-day-a-week in bed, doctor's order, so that she could continue to "tramp for the Lord." She was by then, I believe, in her eighties.

As we entered the bedroom she stretched out her hands to us with a warm, welcoming smile. We asked for more of her story.

"Oh, I've had a very happy life! I've been single because the Lord chose single life for me. I had said, 'I'm yours, Lord, lock, stock, and barrel!' I prayed for victory over the sex life and Jesus gave it."

We spoke of the meaning of suffering. "American Christians are open and eager," she said, "but they do not understand the suffering they must undergo. Christians in Communist countries are much happier. They have to be genuine because of the terrible price they must pay."

I asked how we ought to prepare for suffering.

"Soak in the Word!" was her answer. I was glad for that, for I have

often been asked why I speak and write so often about suffering. There are more than a hundred references to suffering in the New Testament alone.

"I learned of my heavenly Father's love through my own father," Corrie said. "When as a child I couldn't sleep he would put his big hand over my little face. In prison I would say to the Lord, 'Father, just put Your big hand over my little face.' Then I could sleep."

Did she like the movie about her life, *The Hiding Place?*

"Yes, but of course only about one one-hundredth of the suffering was shown."

Because I speak often in public I wondered if she might sometimes feel as I do: Is it right to tell the same story over and over? What if my audience were to say, "Has she got nothing else to talk about except things that happened decades ago?" Her answer comforted me.

"Oh, yes! I dreaded that criticism. But I spoke to my Father— I must have something new! But He said, 'That is the story I gave you. You tell that story!' No, it is humbling to have to say the same thing."

And what of earthly honor?

"If He gives grace, He may give honor too. But I always remember the donkey—he was not proud. He knew that the palms and hosannas were not for him. They were for Jesus! So when I'm given compliments I make a little bouquet of them at the end of the day, and I give my bouquet to Jesus."

Her secretary served us tea and biscuits as we talked about many things. Then Corrie suddenly jumped out of bed and ran (in her purple silk pajamas) over to her suitcase. She took out a square of satin which she held up so that we saw nothing that could be called a pattern, only a jumble of colored threads. Turning it over she showed us a beautifully embroidered gold crown on a purple background. Then she repeated from memory the lovely words of Grant Colfax Tullar, entitled "The Weaver":

My life is but a weaving betwixt the Lord and me,
I do not choose the color—He worketh steadily.
Ofttimes He weaveth sorrow and I in foolish pride,
Forget He sees the upper, and I the underside.
Not till the loom is silent, and the shuttle cease to
    fly
Shall God unroll the canvas and explain the reason
    why.
The dark threads are as needful in the Weaver's
    skillful hand
As the threads of gold and silver in the pattern He
    has planned.

She inscribed her book *In My Father's House* for me and *The Hiding Place* for Val. We left there knowing we had been with a true saint and prophet. It was an especially crucial juncture in my life. My one and only child was about to leave for college, an event filled with joyful anticipation for her but a great mixture of sorrow and joy for a mother. I was a widow then, and dear Corrie, such a glad and strong soldier for Christ, was a very special messenger for me at a crossroad.

How blessed I have been in my life to have known many true soldiers of the Cross. I cannot count them but I know that my mother's guest book holds the names of people from forty-two countries and twenty-four nationalities. We grew up on missionary stories. So I take the admonition of the writer to the Hebrews:

"We want each of you to show this same diligence to the very end, in order to make your hope sure. We do not want you to become lazy, but to imitate those who through faith and patience inherit what has been promised" (Hebrews 6:11-12).

Keep your lives free from the love of money and be content with what you have, because God has said, "Never will I leave you; never will I forsake you." So we say with confidence, "The Lord is my helper; I will not be afraid. What can man do to me?" Remember your leaders, who spoke the word of God to you. Consider the outcome of their way of life and imitate their faith. Jesus Christ is the same yesterday and today and forever.

HEBREWS 13:5-8

Whatever may be troubling you at this moment is not new to the Lord Jesus. He is not taken by surprise. He is *the same*—in a prison cell in World War II and in the midst of your dilemma. It is not a dilemma to Him. Consider the outcome of Corrie's life. Jesus is the same for you. He is not going to leave you. The negative in verse six in the original is more powerful than the English language can express.

When Billy Graham on one of his television broadcasts interviewed Jeanette Clift George, who played the part of Corrie in *The Hiding Place,* he asked what characteristic of her personality seemed most outstanding. Without a moment's hesitation Jeanette answered "Joy! It was her *joy!*" What was the source of that joy? Was it because Corrie was blessed with an unusual optimism, or because things had always worked out so nicely for her? It was far from that. She had learned the meaning of Paul's words in 2 Corinthians 4:15-18:

> All this is for your benefit.... Therefore we do not lose heart. Though outwardly we are wasting away, yet inwardly we are being renewed day by day. For our light and momentary troubles are achieving for us an eternal glory that far outweighs them all. So we fix our eyes not on what is seen, but on what is unseen. For what is seen is temporary, but what is unseen is eternal.

She followed her Master, fixing her eyes on Him "who for the *joy* set before him endured the cross, scorning its shame, and sat down at the right hand of the throne of God. Consider him who endured such opposition from sinful men, so that you will not grow weary and lose heart" (Hebrews 12:2-3).

When the Music Stops

*T*here are sometimes spaces in our lives that seem empty and silent. Things grind to a halt for one reason or another. Not long ago, in the space of a few days, the "music" in my life seemed to stop because of a rejection, a loss, and what seemed to me at the time a monumental failure. I was feeling rather desolate when I came across a paragraph written more than a hundred years ago by the artist John Ruskin:

There is no music in a rest, but there is the making of music in it. In our whole life-melody, the music is broken off here and there by "rests," and we foolishly think we have come to the end of time. God sends a time of forced leisure—sickness, disappointed plans, frustrated efforts—and makes us a sudden pause in the choral hymn of our lives and we lament that our voices must be silent, and our part missing in the music which ever goes up to the ear of the Creator. How does the musician read the rest? See him beat time with unvarying count and catch up the next note true and steady, as if no breaking place had come between. Not without design does God write the music of our lives. But be it ours to learn the time and not be dismayed at the "rests." They are not to be slurred over, nor to be omitted, not to destroy the melody, not to change the keynote. If we look up, God Himself will beat time for us. With the eye on Him we shall strike the next note full and clear.

So the Lord brought to me precisely the word I needed at the moment: There was "the making of music" in what seemed a hollow emptiness. It's His song, not mine, that I'm here to sing. It's His will, not mine, that I'm here to do. Let me focus my vision unwaveringly on Him who alone knows the complete score, "and in the night his song shall be with me" (Psalm 42:8, KJV).

The following was given to me many years ago by my dear Aunt Anne Howard. I wish I knew the author:

Help me to live this day quietly, easily;
To lean upon Thy great strength trustfully,
    restfully;
To meet others peacefully, joyously;
To face tomorrow confidently, courageously.

Injustice

*W*hat to do when you've been hurt and feel sure you didn't "deserve" it?

Any who long for holiness must learn that that quality cannot be merely "bestowed" on us. Holiness is a lifetime process which requires suffering. Our human response is to avoid it in any way we can.

James, "a servant of God and of the Lord Jesus Christ," writes in his epistle (James 1:2-4): "Consider it pure joy, my brothers, whenever you face trials of many kinds, because you know that the testing of your faith develops perseverance. Perseverance must finish its work so that you may be mature and complete, not lacking anything." If you think of those who have most deeply influenced your spiritual life, you will discover that every one of them has suffered, often in ways which seem greatly "undeserved." If it is accident or illness we may label it merely "fate," but if it is wrong done to them by a human being it seems highly "unfair." Were you to ask them what they had learned in the deep waters and the hot fires (see Isaiah 43:2), they would tell you that they had recognized the testing of their *faith*, which had produced, through the grace of God, perseverance. The process is necessary for all of us. Christ Himself experienced far more hurts, injustice, and pure hatred than you and I will ever know. "During the days of Jesus' life on earth, he offered up prayers and petitions with loud cries and tears to the one who could save him from death, and he was heard because of his reverent submission. Although he was a son, he *learned obedience from what he suffered* and once made perfect, he became the source of eternal salvation for all who obey him" (Hebrews: 5:7-9).

Dare we suppose that we do not need the lessons of suffering? Shall we refuse to take up the cross and follow our Lord and Master? My friend Arlita Winston who teaches a group of pastors' wives, gave me what she calls "the Balm of Gilead," four simple (not *easy!*) steps toward peace when we have been wronged—perhaps even outraged—and are convinced we didn't deserve it:

1. *Confess* (my anger, hatred, desire for revenge, self-pity ...). Both I and the one wronged me now need the same Cross—the Cross on which our sinless Savior suffered.
2. *Repent.* This is a 180-degree turnaround.
3. *Pray,* "Wash me with Your blood, cleanse me."
4. *Bless* the one who hurt you. Forgive him and bless him!

"Dear friends, do not be surprised at the painful trial you are suffering, as though something strange were happening to you. But rejoice that you participate in the sufferings of Christ, so that you may be overjoyed when his glory is revealed" (1 Peter 4:12-13).

Suffering is a gift. "It has been granted to you on behalf of Christ not only to believe on him, but also to suffer for him, since you are going through the same struggle you saw I had, and now hear that I still have" (Philippians 1:29-30). Fénelon (1651-1715) said, "Accustom yourself to unreasonableness and injustice. Abide in peace in the presence of God, who sees all these evils more clearly than you do, and who permits them. Be content with doing with calmness the little which depends upon yourself, and let all else be to you as if it were not."

"Now if we are children, then we are heirs—heirs of God and co-heirs with Christ, if indeed we share in his sufferings in order that we may also share in his glory. I consider that our present sufferings are not worth comparing with the glory that will be revealed in us" (Romans 8:17-18).

Jesus told us that if we *want* to be disciples, we must *deny ourselves* (give up all right to ourselves), *take up the cross* (which is "no great action done once for all; it consists in the continual practice of small duties which are distasteful to us"—J.H. Newman), and we must *follow* Him. May He grant to us the grace to do these painful but wonderfully liberating things! And may we never forget the *joy* which follows obedience. Trust and obey—there's no other way to be happy.

As I look back over a long life I can see that whenever I have disobeyed, it has led sooner or later to misery. Whenever I have obeyed, it had led to peace and joy, even though the path of obedience has sometimes entailed suffering.

"O Lord, you are my God; I will exalt you and praise your name, for in perfect faithfulness you have done marvelous things, things planned long ago" (Isaiah 25:1).

Joy to the World

hanksgiving and Christmas (now called "Turkey Day" and "Sparkletime" by some, alas!) are holidays that are supposed to be happy. When there is no one to thank and the Christ of Christmas is unknown, there may be a measure of happiness—if the dinner is as delectable as hoped, and the relatives manage to treat each other fairly civilly. But how many stories we hear of bleak and miserable family get-togethers—and the vows, "Never again!"

A holiday is a holy day, meant to be hallowed—meant also to hallow the rest of life. Alexander Schmemann says that to the man of the past, "a feast was not merely a 'break' in an otherwise meaningless and hard life of work, but a *justification* of that work, its fruit, its—so to speak—transformation into joy and therefore into freedom. A feast was thus always deeply and organically related to time, to the natural cycles of times, to the whole framework of man's life in the world. And, whether we want it or not, whether we like it or not, Christianity accepted and made its own this fundamentally human phenomenon of feast, as it *accepted* and made its own the whole man and all of his needs. But, as in everything else, Christians accepted the feast not only by giving it a new meaning, by transforming its 'content,' but by taking it, along with the whole of 'natural' man, through death and resurrection...."

Schmemann points out a strange paradox here: Christianity

is, on one hand, the *end* of all natural joy, "because by revealing the perfect man it revealed the abyss of man's alienation from God.... Since the Gospel was preached in this world all attempts to go back to a pure 'pagan joy,' all 'renaissances,' all 'healthy optimisms' were bound to fail. 'There is but one sadness,' said Leon Bloy, 'that of not being a saint.' And it is this sadness that permeates mysteriously the whole life of the world, its frantic and pathetic hunger and thirst for perfection, which kills all joy.... Christianity was the revelation and the gift of joy ... and thus, the gift of genuine feast" *(For the Life of the World)*.

Have we Christians accepted the "whole ethos of our joyless and business-minded culture," relegating joy to the category of "fun," "relaxation," or a time for "winding down"? Do we know much of true joy, or does the word frighten us? Do we look at it with suspicion in the world which Wordsworth said is a world of "getting and spending," where "we lay waste our powers"? Life is punctuated here and there with a little happiness. We give ourselves permission to have fun and then wonder if we had any. We try to relax and tomorrow's business constricts our hearts. Gerard Manley Hopkins asks, "Why are we so haggard at the heart, so care-coiled, so fagged, so fashed, so cogged, so cumbered?"

Fest means *joy.* Joy is the keynote of the Christian life. It is not something that happens. It is a *gift,* given to us in the coming of Christ. A few humble shepherds, doing their routine sheep-watching duty in the fields near Bethlehem one night, were astounded when an angel appeared. There was no question about it—it was an angel all right, and the glory of the Lord encompassed the shepherds. They were terrified. But the angel brought good news of great joy, meant not only for them but for all people throughout the world. (Had you thought that Mary and Joseph did not hear the angels' song? DeSales suggests that they only heard the child weep, "and saw, by the little light borrowed from some wretched lamp, the eyes of this divine child all filled with tears, and faint under the rigor of the cold.")

When Mary still carried the Babe in her womb, it did not take her long to hurry to the home of her cousin Elisabeth (yes, the King James Version has an s in that name!), who was herself miraculously pregnant in her old age. Perhaps it was while Mary talked with the older woman that she was enabled to grasp a new aspect of the solemn mystery she bore in her womb. This child was her Savior! She His mother, and He her Redeemer, and she was filled with joy, and sang about it in the beautiful Magnificat, "My soul doth magnify the Lord, and my spirit hath rejoiced in God my Savior" (Luke 1:46-47, KJV).

God gives to us a heavenly gift called joy, radically different in quality from any natural joy. John the Baptist, knowing that Jesus was now to be the greater and he the lesser, was full of joy at hearing the Bridegroom's voice. When Jesus was about to leave His disciples, He gave them His own joy, in order that their joy might be complete. The apostle Paul, chained in prison, wrote to the Philippians the Epistle of Joy. When the apostle Peter was writing to exiles ("strangers in the world"), he reminded them that although they had had to suffer grief in all kinds of trials, these had come so that their faith might be proved genuine and might "result in praise, glory and honor when Jesus Christ is revealed. Though you have not seen him, you love him; and even though you do not see him now, you believe in him and are filled with an inexpressible and glorious joy, for you are receiving the goal of your faith, the salvation of your souls" (1 Peter 1:7-9).

And throughout the millennia Christians who have known deep suffering have found at the same time the gift of joy. Suffering and joy are not mutually exclusive. Little Fanny Crosby, blinded at six weeks because of a doctor's mistake, wrote when she was only nine,

> O what a happy soul am I, although I cannot see!
> I am resolved that in this world contented I will be.
> How many blessings I enjoy that other people don't!
> To weep and sigh because I'm blind, I cannot and I won't.

The joy of the Lord was her strength.

Love and obedience are the secrets of true joy. "Joy," wrote C.S. Lewis, "is the serious business of heaven." I love that, and I am sure it must be true, for heaven is peopled with those who want no other business but to love God and to manifest that love, perfectly and continuously, by a glad obedience. Jesus said, "If you obey my commands, you will remain in my love, just as I have obeyed my Father's commands and remain in his love. I have told you this so that my joy may be in you and that your joy may be complete" (John 15:10-11).

Holidays then, for us who love God, are not mere "time out" from work days. They are a celebration of the gift of work itself, days on which we celebrate work by declaring our freedom. In a manner of speaking we announce that on this one day we may rest from our work and, without pressure or guilt, we may be glad. A holiday is a holy day—meant for rejoicing in God.

Perhaps we will want to pray the words of Jeremy Taylor, "Lord, do Thou turn me all into love, and all my love into obedience, and may my obedience be without interruption." Love equals joy which equals peace.

The Grand Lesson

Give thanks in all circumstances, for this is God's will for you in Christ Jesus" (1 Thessalonians 5:18). It is the apostle Paul who speaks so unequivocally to us: *no matter in what circumstances we find ourselves.* His words are not empty. He had endured hard work, imprisonments, floggings, exposure to death again and again, five times had received forty lashes minus one. He was beaten with rods, stoned, shipwrecked three times, had spent a night and a day in the open sea and was constantly on the move. He knew dangers from rivers, bandits, his own countrymen and Gentiles, dangers in the country, at sea, and from false brothers. He had labored and toiled, gone without sleep, suffered hunger, thirst, scant food, cold, and nakedness.

He boasted of things that showed his weakness, and perhaps the most ignominious experience of all was his having to be lowered over a wall in a basket—of all things!

Paul was no stranger to suffering. "The God and Father of the Lord Jesus, who is to be praised forever," he said, "knows that I am not lying."

All of us have had some brush with suffering, at least if you accept my simple definition: *having what you don't want or wanting what you don't have.*

If you discover that the washing machine has just quit, you have what you don't want—a useless mechanism—but it is a mere "Oh no!" sort of thing which we would never dignify by using the word *suffering.*

If, however, you learn that someone has just filed a lawsuit against you, the "Oh No!" may be the beginning of many sorrows. You have what you don't want. Let us not fail to recognize that this is one of the many forms of suffering.

Suppose you have lost your job or your house. You suffer. If someone very dear to you has just died, you greatly miss what you no longer have.

Paul said, "I consider that our present sufferings are not worth comparing with the glory that will be revealed in us. The creation waits in eager expectation for the sons of God to be revealed. For the creation was subjected to frustration, not by its own choice, but by the will of the one who subjected it" (Romans 8:18-20).

The apostle had received mysterious revelations. He had known a man caught up to Paradise, but was not allowed to talk about it. He wanted no one to think more of him than was warranted. But the supreme test, that which seemed most likely to stagger the faithful apostle, was a very small thing indeed—a mere thorn.

> To keep me from becoming conceited because of these surpassingly great revelations, there was given me a thorn in my flesh, a messenger of Satan, to torment me. Three times I pleaded with the Lord to take it away from me. [Had He not done so, you and I would never have learned the grand lesson:] *My grace is all you need, for power comes to its full strength in weakness.*
>
> 2 CORINTHIANS 12:7-9, italics mine

God in Each Moment

The coming of the Savior of the world was not announced with ticker tape and balloons. There was the blazing splendor of the Lord and the sudden appearance of a vast host of the armies of heaven with their stunning piece of news—but how many saw? How many heard? No one, it seems, in the little town of Bethlehem—only a group of humble shepherds out on the dewy hillside. They were not thrilled or excited by the heavenly display. They were terror-stricken.

Bethlehem was crowded that night. There was the hustle and bustle of travelers looking for lodging. In the inns, noise, frustration, drunkenness, argument. Hidden from all, in back of one of the inns, knelt a young woman in the agony of giving birth.

The Virgin Mary and her husband, Joseph, had welcomed with open arms, nine months before, what without faith they would have dreaded and avoided. Each day had brought its further testings. Imagine their receiving news, when her time was near, that a trek to far-off Bethlehem was demanded by law at such a time! Fancy Joseph's finding no room for her now that she was in labor. Few comforts were theirs that night, but faith sustained them. There was nowhere to lean except the Everlasting Arms. They had God's word, specially delivered by the angel Gabriel. Weak things, lowly things, painful things, silent things—the instinct of their faith told them God was in all of these. They *knew,* because God had given them His word.

Therefore they moved trustfully, quietly, through each moment, God being in charge, God being *in* that moment.

And so it may be for us when God's order is the reverse of what we expect. He is *in* each moment, *in* us, *with* us, as He is with the holy couple on their wearisome journey over the dusty roads and in the raw cattle shed. Should we expect to see how things are working together for our good? No, not yet. We see not yet. We only *know*. Joseph and Mary, lacking faith, would surely have felt that things were working strongly against them.

> Ah! The poverty, the humility of God reduced to lying on straw in a manger, crying and trembling and breaking Mary's noble heart. Ask the inhabitants of Bethlehem what they think; if that child had been born in a palace in princely surroundings they would worship him, But ask Mary, Joseph, the magi, the priest, and they will tell you that they see in this dire poverty something which makes God more glorious, more adorable. What is deprivation to the senses nourishes and strengthens faith. The less there is for the senses, the more there is for the soul.
>
> (Jean-Pierre de Caussade)

In the barren places of my life I can be assured that God is there as He is when life is fruitful, and that the time is coming (give me patience, Lord, to wait!) when He will fulfill His word: "I will put in the desert the cedar and the acacia, the myrtle and the olive. I will set pines in the wasteland, the fir and the cypress together, so that people may see and know, may consider and understand, that the hand of the Lord has done this" (Isaiah 41:19-20).

Like little children on Christmas Eve, we *know* that lovely surprises are in the making. We can't see them. We have simply been told, and we believe. *Tomorrow we shall see.*

"Almighty God, Who canst give the light that in darkness shall make us glad, the life that in gloom shall make us joy, and the peace that amidst discord shall bring us quietness! Let us live this day in that light, that life, and that peace, so that we may gain the victory over those things that press us down, and over the flesh that so often encumbers us, and over death that seemeth for a moment to win the victory. Thus we, being filled with inward peace, and light, and life, may walk all the days of this our mortal life, doing our work as the business of our Father, glorifying it because it is Thy will, knowing that what Thou givest Thou givest in love. Bestow upon us the greatest and last blessing, that we, being in Thy presence, may be life unto Thee for evermore. These things we do ask, in the name of Jesus Christ our Lord. Amen." (George Dawson, 1821-1876)

Six

of

Marriage, Courtship, and Singleness

On Being Single

Several years ago at a convention I fell into conversation with a radiantly lovely single woman named Michelle—clearly a woman of God. I asked her to jot down some thoughts on her life as a single.

"I am very rich. I often describe myself as a mouse sitting in the middle of a cheesecake. I don't know where to bite next. I was very frightened about where I should live and what I would do. I had always imagined I would marry before college was over but that was not to be. When I expressed my concern to my father he had me sit down and list priorities for my life after college. It was a big decision to move to Minnesota while my parents were in Florida, but a very wise one as I have found a richer life than I could imagine. Now on being single:

"'We should offer the Lord the sacrifice of Abel. Let it be a sacrifice of young, unblemished flesh, the best of the flock, of a healthy and holy flesh: a sacrifice of hearts that have one love alone: You, my God. Let it be a sacrifice of minds that have been shaped through deep study and will surrender to Your wisdom; of childlike souls who will think only of pleasing You'" (*The Forge*, J. Escriva).

"As single people we must be willing to offer these younger years of ours to the Lord, not waiting for our life circumstances to change. We may be more free now than we will ever be in active service for God. If He chooses to have us married some day that is His business. Ours is to look to Him and serve Him now. He can use our youth to reach an increasingly more spiritually needy teenage and preteen world. We can give hope to the elderly who see very little evidence of faith around them. We can serve our family and friends by lightening their loads. The example we give of competent work will help others to improve their own work. Our profession will become a pedestal for Christ so that He can be seen even by those who are far away. We can also take this time to prepare ourselves to be brides—if not earthly brides, heavenly ones.

"When people ask if my biological clock is not ticking now that I am twenty-nine, I laugh. Four of my best friends have nineteen children collectively. I have four godchildren and many other children at church and in my neighborhood—many opportunities to 'mother.' Last Saturday I had twelve children overnight at my house. Between midnight, 2:00 A.M. and 5:00 A.M. feeding of the babies, and quieting and caring for the older ones, I couldn't have heard any biological clock ticking even if there was one!

"My encouragement to singles who want to marry: Invest in the marriages of others. Lighten their load. Cook meals for new mothers. Take the children on special outings so parents can have time together. Serve and you won't have time for discontent. Love and your heart will be filled with the love of others. 'Give and it will be given to you, pressed down and running over.'

"I was courted by a wonderful young man during my college days. He possessed all of the qualities of the husband I wished for. All we needed was the go-ahead that this was God's plan for our lives. For three years we heard God saying *wait.* Then the answer was clear: *no.* It was not only clear, it was final. I knew I had to 'get a life.' God would help me but He would not drop it into my lap. I bought a house, opened a small business. I had a gift for homemaking, rented three extra rooms to Christian single women who filled my home with life, prayer, and activity. Together we prayed, shared, gardened, and decorated 'our' home. When each married and moved on, my house became 'home' to a multitude of children, neighbors, and church friends. About every third weekend different friends' children come to stay while the parents get away for marriage renewal time.

"I am *very* glad now that I did not wait around till I was married to 'get a life.' Life has been happening all around me these past years and many of my greatest experiences have been entering deeply into life with others. Here is a favorite quote: "The pathway to holiness is located right where you are. In those circumstances, those relationships, in that tiredness, in that challenge. The grace of God to make you holy is right there.'"

May God use Michelle's example to deliver others (not by any means necessarily singles) from self-pity and to remind them of the words of the Lord Jesus in Matthew 25:40: "Whatever you did for one of the least of these brothers, you did for me." Ask Him. He will show you what to do.

Don't Do It

Today's so-called freedom of choice often leads not to freedom but to crushing bondage. Take, for example, the freedom the world offers in its motto JUST DO IT! A radio listener wrote of her own devastating experience of those shackles, and begged me to pass on her story.

"At seventeen years of age I chose to rebel against God and entered a relationship with my boyfriend that delivered not happiness but guilt and grief. I 'fell in love' and rather than trust God, I went after the object of my desire with all the wiles and passions of a teen-age romantic. At first what we did 'felt good'—for the moment. I tried pushing my guilt into a closet and shutting the door, but kept on doing what came naturally. I remember thinking even then, 'What will you say to your daughter some day if she asks, "Were you a virgin when you got married?"' Over the years that question has come to mind time and time again.

"The day before the wedding my fiancé forced himself on me, and never having said NO before, I felt helpless to stop him. All these years later I still feel the hurt and violation of that moment. There was no tenderness, no love, only desire, lust, passion.

"How could I have known the repercussions through the years of that one decision on my part to have my own way and not God's. I realize what a precious, holy gift we so thoughtlessly threw away in our youth. And now I have had to ask my daughter, 'Are you pregnant?' and hear her tearful reply 'Yes.' I cannot express in words the deep wound to my soul this has caused. Although I did not make her decisions for her, I see that by my actions and choices so many years ago I left her spiritually vulnerable to Satan's onslaught.

"If only I could look each teenage girl in the eye and tell her, 'There are consequences to every moral decision you make; there are repercussions that will follow you the rest of your life and into the next generation!'

"How I yearn to look each teenage boy in the eye and tell him, 'Be strong. Be a real man. Trust God's word, discipline yourself, don't give in to youthful lust and trade your birthright of godly love for a mess of pottage that will turn to ashes in your heart.'

"I have learned too late the truth I heard a man of God say: 'Love can always wait to give. Lust can never wait to get.'

"And you know—it's funny (*sad*) not a single time did those stolen moments of passion and lust bring real pleasure to me, either physically or emotionally."

The Bible is perfectly clear on this matter. God has given the guidelines which lead to true fulfillment and joy.

"Brothers, we instructed you how to live in order to please God, as in fact you are living. Now we ask you and urge you in the Lord Jesus to do this more and more. For you know what instructions we gave you by the authority of the Lord Jesus. It is God's will that you should be sanctified: that you should avoid sexual immorality; that each of you should learn to control his own body in a way that is holy and honorable, not in passionate lust like the heathen, who do not know God…. God did not call us to be impure, but to live a holy life. Therefore, he who rejects this instruction does not reject man but God, who gives you his Holy Spirit" (1 Thessalonians 4:1-8).

A Disaster Aborted

A subscriber to my newsletter found herself pregnant. Devastated, she felt she could not possibly handle more than her three children. Her husband agreed. She had had difficult pregnancies and had needed hospitalization. "I knew that pregnancy would be a huge disruption and had many horrible thoughts about aborting the baby, and although I had been strongly pro-life I now felt that an exception had to be made. I called the clinic, scheduled an appointment, thinking I could keep it a secret and would have to keep it for the rest of my life. I knew I would have to answer for my sin, but felt so angry and desperate—I would be the only one to pay the price and I would be willing to live with it.

"On one of the dark days that followed I read your newsletter—an article called 'Don't Do It.' One line stabbed me to the heart. A woman had chosen to give away her virginity before she was married and now her daughter had done the same. I realized in an instant that that was a price I was not willing to pay—I would not have my children pay for my sin. I talked to my husband and we cried many tears but determined in our hearts to do what is right. I called the clinic, canceled the appointment. Sickness came as expected but I survived! My baby arrived and we put the verse from Jeremiah on her birth announcement, 'You are loved with an everlasting love.'

"I hold her now and she looks at me with her little blue eyes and I love her in a way that I never thought I could. I have cried oceans of tears thinking about what I could have done in a rash moment and the unbearable pain I would have had to live with for the rest of my life. I have a new empathy for women who feel that they are in a 'crisis' pregnancy, but I also am more firmly convinced that if a person feels that pregnancy is a mistake, *killing the baby won't fix it.* The pain and repercussions from that decision would go on forever—beyond my lifetime, to my children, grandchildren, and great-grandchildren. I am so thankful to the Lord for His mercy in searing my heart with the truth and for keeping me from doing something I would have regretted forever. I thought you would want to know."

Yes, dear lady, I am so glad. May the Lord make you an instrument of His peace to other fearful prospective mothers.

The Hazards of Homemade Vows

Many engaged couples today love the idea of writing their own wedding vows and many a minister finds no reason to persuade them otherwise. I think it was about thirty-five years ago that improvisation was introduced—a sunny California meadow, a barefoot bride wearing wildflowers in her hair, and a groom dressed like Ghandi, reading what he hopes is poetry. Things slid ignominiously downhill. At the conclusion of his own marriage a Rev. Mr. Gould of Chicago turned to his bride and said, "Thank you for choosing an outrageous cuss like me." His bride burst out laughing. The formality of bridal gowns and rent-a-tuxes underlines the incongruity of such events. My husband Lars attended what might be called a fun nuptial. As the groomsmen chanted, "The ring! The ring! Who's got the ring?" down the aisle came a large and reluctant dog with the ring attached to his collar.

Marriage is not a private transaction. It ought never to be a mere *concoction*. It is public business as the couple joins the enterprise of the human race. The vow creates the couple, not the couple the vow. Why would a Christian bride refuse the time-honored vow, "I, *N.*, take thee, *M.*, to be my wedded husband, to have and to hold from this day forward, for better for worse, for richer for poorer, in sickness and in health, to love and to cherish, and to obey, till death us do part, according to God's holy ordinance; and thereto I give thee my troth"? It is as G.K.

Chesterton wrote, "[The opponents of vows) appear to imagine that the ideal of constancy was a yoke mysteriously imposed on mankind by the devil, instead of being, as it is, a yoke consistently imposed by all lovers on themselves. They have invented a phrase, a phrase that is a black and white contradiction in two words—'free-love'—as if a lover ever had been or ever could be, free.... It is exactly this back-door, this sense of having a retreat behind us, that is, to our minds, the sterilizing spirit in modern pleasure. Everywhere there is the persistent and insane attempt to obtain pleasure without paying for it.... Thus, in religion and morals, the decadent mystics say, 'Let us have the fragrance of sacred purity without the sorrow of self-restraint'.... Thus, in love, the free-lovers say, 'Let us have the splendor of offering ourselves without the peril of committing ourselves; let us see whether one cannot commit suicide an unlimited number of times.'

"Emphatically it will not work. There are thrilling moments doubtless, for the spectator, the amateur, and the aesthete; but there is one thrill that is known only to the soldier who fights for his own flag, to the ascetic who starves himself for his own illumination, to the lover who makes finally his own choice. And it is this transfiguring self-discipline that makes the vow a truly sane thing."

If the prospective bride and groom read earnestly Chesterton's remarks, will they still have the temerity to cobble up their own vows?

Letter to a Twelve-Year-Old

*I*t is a great thing to me that you felt free to write and tell me about holding hands with Ronnie. The fact that it was exciting to you, and you wanted to tell me about it, makes me know that it is significant in your life, and I am glad that you share with me things that mean something to you. You were not quite sure, you said, that I would "approve." I can't remember what I have said to you on the subject but I have tried to help you understand who you are and the value of your person—soul and body.

Holding hands is a way of showing friendship but a little warmer friendship than "ordinary," perhaps. To touch a boy, at your age, is, as you say, "exciting." This is because you are becoming a woman, and physical contact with a man usually is, for a woman, exciting to a degree. This is the way God arranged things, and I think it was a pretty marvelous idea of His—one I would never have had the courage to go through with if I had been the Creator, because it is also terribly dangerous! It is dangerous because it is a power—the sexual instinct is like the power of electricity. It has its proper uses, and they are very valuable and helpful indeed, but if not carefully controlled it can be deadly. So this is where *maturity* comes in. You are not yet mature, and what you have recently learned is that you have a response to the opposite sex, and it's fun. I'm glad for that. It is not a bad thing at all. But because you are a person—a human being, made in the image of *God*, whom God *loves*—and not an animal, you are worth something, and you ought never to give away things that have great value without first thinking very carefully what they are worth, and making sure that you want to make this kind of gift.

Now, holding hands is not quite the same as "giving yourself away," of course, but it is giving a part of yourself. Any expression of friendship is a gift. And the more you give, the higher the price you pay, and the more certain you must be of what it is you are doing.

Unfortunately many young people have no idea whatsoever of themselves as persons, much less of God's idea of them or of His love and care. These are things you know very well, and have been taught since you were very small. Many young people have no conception of giving themselves. They are concerned with what they can *get*. "What will *I* get out of this? Will this satisfy *me?* Where can I have a good time?" You know the sort of thing.

In your relationships with boys from now on until you get married, I earnestly hope and pray that you will remember who it is that you belong to first of all—to the Lord, of course. He made you, He bought you, He loves you more than anyone ever will. Your body is a precious thing—the expression of who you are, the only place in which your personality is manifest and in which you can serve the Lord.

Perhaps one day the Lord will *give* you in marriage to a man who loves you, to be his until death parts you, and on that day you will be thankful if you have saved yourself for him. You know, I think that I never held hands with any boy until I fell in love with your father. No boy ever kissed me; not until your father asked me to marry him did he kiss me. Everyone thought I was crazy. Your daddy did not think so when he learned that he was the first. He was terribly glad, although he *had* thought I was a little stuffy to make him wait until we were engaged to kiss me!

It is a funny thing, but it is a fact, that boys are more interested in a girl who keeps a little distance. There is something about *un*availability which enhances one's desire—like Eve and the apple, you know. The one fruit which God said she could not taste, she had to have. It's human nature. So don't be too "easy to get." Don't be cheap. Word gets around pretty fast among the boys about which girls *will* and which ones *won't.* But never think for a second that the girls who *will* are the ones boys like best, or respect, or would want for a wife. It isn't so. You have plenty of time, don't forget. You are only twelve, and you won't get married for eight years or more. Life gets suddenly terribly thrilling and exciting and interesting and scary, and you want to get on the toboggan and roar off with the rest of them. Don't do it. Sit down. Think. Pray. Ponder who and what you are. Take account of the things that really matter, and what you want of life. Save yourself for your husband, for the Lord. Be simple and natural and unselfish and free and friendly, by all means. But let the boys know you are *different.* This will sometimes take a lot of discipline and courage and maybe even sacrifice. Are you willing for that?

Do me the favor of reading Romans 12:1-2 in the PHILLIPS translation: "With eyes wide open to the mercies of God, I beg you, my brothers, as an act of intelligent worship, to give him your bodies, as a living sacrifice, consecrated to him and acceptable by him. Don't let the world around you squeeze you into its own mold, but let God remold your minds from within, so that you may prove in practice that the plan of God for you is good, meets all his demands and moves toward the goal of true maturity."

Now sit down and write me what you think about what I've said! You know that I say it because I love you and have great hopes for you and believe in you and am more thankful to God that you can possibly imagine for His having given you to me. With a heartful of love, your Mama.

The Story of a Courtship

*I*n 1992 I received a letter from Robert, who wondered if God might be asking him to lay down his love for Amy in order to serve as a missionary. I wrote, "I am praying for you and Amy on this gray and rather wintry spring day in Massachusetts.... Go on doing the things that you know God is calling you to do today, and in His time He will make crystal clear the decision about marriage."

Robert and Amy had offered their love for each other as Abraham had offered Isaac, laying him on the altar, trusting God to do with the sacrifice as He saw fit. At Christmas, 1994, they felt Him "breathing life into our relationship once again." Robert took Amy to hear a visiting speaker in a church. "I wanted to show her the letter that lady had written to me, and of course I wanted to bring Amy up to talk to her afterwards. I had no idea, however, what was about to happen."

He was exhausted that night and heard little of the talk on Simplicity. But God seemed to make every word "come alive" in Amy's heart.

"You gave short, sharp answers to difficult questions, but I was so thankful to hear you untangle the complications and point out the simplicity of the answer. Robert and I still talk about 'doing the next thing,' and 'getting up early begins the night before.'" Robert's version of that evening:

"Here Amy and I are, waiting in line where people had their

books for Elisabeth to autograph. We had no book and I had not brought the letter she wrote me, so I wasn't exactly sure what we were going to say to her.

"I spoke first. 'Mrs. Elliot, I wanted to thank you for your ministry and the books you have written because several years ago, you wrote me a letter about a girl I was seeing, and she is here tonight.'

"Mrs. Elliot smiled, 'Oh really? Where is she?'

"'Right here.' Amy came and knelt beside me.

"'Are you married yet?' Elisabeth said, looking pleasantly at the two of us.

"'Well uh, not yet,' I replied, rather embarrassed, 'but I believe God will be faithful.'

"'What are you waiting for?' Elisabeth looked at me.

"I had no answer.

"She repeated her question, 'Well, what are you waiting for?'

"I knew the time was right. Right there, on our knees there in the presence of Elisabeth Elliot and God's sovereign smile, I asked Amy to marry me. It was wonderful. God is wonderful. Amy is wonderful, and that was just the confirmation I needed to marry her."

Weeks went by. One day I said to Lars, "I wonder what ever happened to that sweet couple we met in Arkansas—remember the man who proposed in the foyer of the church? I *do* hope they got married!"

It was only a day or two later that we received a letter from Amy, enclosing the above account from Robert. "He loves to tell this story," she wrote. "I want to thank you for prompting

Robert to propose to me. I have never seen him so happy, He is still giddy at the thought of becoming my husband, and I cannot express to you how much I love him and want to be his helpmate. I will soon send you an invitation to our wedding. I hope it will bring a smile to your face as it has to ours."

It did. It also sent a huge surge of thanksgiving through my whole soul. Our God is the Wonderful Counselor, able and more than able to bring a man and woman together in His time, in His often mysterious and astonishing ways.

What Does It Mean to Submit?

*J*esus showed us the answer. Yet the question comes again and again. Women choke on it. Philippians 2:5-11 is the divine prescription:

> Your attitude should be the same as that of Christ Jesus: Who, being in very nature God, did not consider equality with God something to be grasped, but made himself nothing, taking the very nature of a servant, being made in human likeness. And being found in appearance as a man, he humbled himself and became obedient to death—even death on a cross! Therefore God exalted him to the highest place and gave him the name that is above every name, that at the name of Jesus every knee should bow, in heaven and on earth and under the earth, and every tongue confess that Jesus Christ is Lord, to the glory of God the Father.

Here is my friend Judith Lake's response to the question of submission:

> I, being made in the image of God—a believer, a woman, and a wife, having equal worth in God's sight and equal access to the Lord as my husband—choose not to grasp after a position of equal leadership with my husband which is not my God-given place. Rather, I choose by God's grace

to make myself nothing, taking on the very nature of a servant which was the attitude of Jesus—desiring with all my heart to be humble like Him. I choose to be obedient to God's command to submit to my husband and die to myself. I understand that this decision will cause pain and suffering at times, but in those moments may I all the more identify with my Lord. When the cross is hard to bear, I pray for the will to give Him the burden of my heart and to learn to rest in Him. I trust God and His Word and am confident that He knows what is best for me. One day He will exalt me in heaven as one of His own who obeyed His will. By His grace, I will receive my reward worshiping Him in His presence forever, confessing Jesus Christ as Lord to the glory of God the Father.

"O Lord, give us such a mighty love for Thee as may sweeten all our obedience. Let us not serve Thee with the spirit of bondage as slaves, but with the cheerfulness and gladness of children in delighting ourselves in Thee and rejoicing in Thy work. Amen." (Benjamin Jenks, 1646-1724)

Verbal Authority

The Bible tells us that children are to obey their parents. In our many travels Lars and I observe that few young parents have any idea that a child *can* be taught to obey. Some of them, alas, feel that it would damage their little egos to correct them. But God's word is clear: "He who spares the rod hates his son, but he who loves him is careful to discipline him." But how to begin?

A young couple asked me to help them learn to discipline their ten-month-old son. We met in a restaurant and, to my dismay, they brought the child with them. My heart sank for I had hoped they would leave him at home so that we might have uninterrupted conversation.

The child was put in a high chair (the kind without an attached tray) at one end of the table. His mother and father were at his right on one side of the table, I at his left. The couple chatted to me and another guest who was at my left. It did not take long before the baby grabbed his mother's fork. Without a word she took it from his hand. He looked around, then reached across her plate for her knife. She took it away. Next was the spoon. She said *nothing*, simply took it out of his hand. He cried, pouted, waited a short time, then reached for her water glass.

By this time the mother was exasperated and helpless. She called the waitress, asked for a glass of milk and some crackers for the child, while the adults read the menu and the child fussed.

When he had finished with crackers and milk he began to eye my spoon. Slowly he moved his left hand toward it. I simply lowered my face to the level of his, looked him kindly in the eye, and said quietly, "Jeremy, no." He withdrew his hand at once and looked at his mother.

She was oblivious. It was evident that she did not *understand* verbal authority, supposing that the child was too young to understand since he was too young to *talk*. A child is usually farther ahead in understanding than most parents realize. Not once had she said *no*.

The meal progressed with some conversation and further grapplings between mother and child. Every now and then the child eyed me, then finally began to very slowly to move his hand once again toward my spoon. This time all I did was look him steadily in the eye. I said nothing. He looked away, pouted, and withdrew his hand.

Jeremy had never seen me before, but he recognized verbal authority. On his right were two helpless young parents, earnestly wanting to do right by their child (or they would not have asked for my help), yet never addressing him by name, never issuing the simple command "No." The interesting thing about this whole scene was that this baby clearly understood that there was no such thing on his right. I am afraid the parents failed to see the lesson I had hoped to show them.

What infinite pains parents would avoid if they would only start early to teach children the meaning of *verbal* authority. As soon as a child can crawl, usually around seven or eight months, he will immediately begin to touch things he ought not to touch:

books, the TV, knickknacks on the coffee table, etc. He will very likely make a beeline for the very thing he is to be taught not to touch. If parents "child proof" the house, putting everything out of the baby's reach, they are teaching him that he may touch anything *within* reach. What happens when he goes to the grocery store or to his Aunt Susie's house? Disaster! "No" and "Come" must be taught at once. Note four things that will help:

1. Speak the child's name in a calm tone of voice.
2. Establish eye contact.
3. Issue a one word command, "No" or "Come."
4. Do not repeat.

The initial lesson will require repetition. It might be wise simply to set aside a whole uninterrupted hour to teach the lesson. Think what infinite pains will be averted for the rest of his growing-up years if he learns thoroughly that Daddy and Mama mean exactly what they say, and they mean it the first time. If a parent makes a habit of repeating commands, he is training the child to delay his obedience. My parents made it clear to us that delayed obedience would be treated as disobedience.

If the children are older and things seem to have gotten a bit out of hand I suggest that you call a family council. Gather everybody together and explain to the children that their parents have made some bad mistakes. Confess to them that you are very sorry about this, you realize that you have not created as happy a home as you want to have, but you have now learned some things and are going to start over. (Your children will be astonished that parents, too, have to learn things!) Then, down on your knees, everyone! Pray for the Lord's forgiveness and ask Him to help you to be what mothers and fathers are supposed to be to their children, and to help the children to do what they ought to do, quickly and cheerfully. Perhaps you will ask each child to pray briefly.

The next step is to make it clear that you are going to expect your children to obey you. It is amazing what can result from a clear understanding of expectations. Depending on the ages of the children, you might want to illustrate the necessity of obedience by referring to the coach of an athletic team—he calls the shots, the players do exactly what he says. If they don't, there's no game. Or point to traffic laws which make it possible for everybody to move in an orderly way, according to the speed laws, and on the right side of the street. If one person runs through a red light he could kill somebody.

Do not despair! Yes, you long to have a peaceful home and it seems that our adversary the devil continually "prowls around like a roaring lion looking for someone to devour" (1 Peter 5:8) But we have a Mighty Fortress, a God who loves us and promises to help us. Things should be done in a Christian home "decently and in order" (1 Corinthians 14:40, KJV).

> Drop Thy still dews of quietness
>> Till all our strivings cease;
> Take from our souls the strain and stress
>> And let our *ordered lives* confess
> The beauty of Thy peace.
>
> (John Greenleaf Whittier)

I know it is possible to have a peaceful home. My parents, who had six children, made it so. My friends Joe and Arlita Winston, parents of five and now grandparents of twenty-three, ordered their home in such a way as to eliminate chaos. Thousands have done it.

"Though we live in the world, we do not wage war as the world does. The weapons we fight with are not the weapons of the world. On the contrary, they have divine power to demolish strongholds. We demolish arguments and every pretension that sets itself up against the knowledge of God, and we take captive every thought to make it obedient to Christ" (2 Corinthians 10:3-5).

Jesus Christ has overcome the world. He can demolish the strongholds that the enemy may have established in your home. My great-grandfather, Henry Clay Trumbull, reared eight children. He wrote a book, *Hints on Child Training,* in which he says, "It is a parent's privilege and it is a parent's duty to make his children, by God's blessing, to be and to do what they should be and do, rather than what they would like to be and do."

Vance Havner, that delightful old Southern preacher, had a good definition of the discipline which works best with a small child: "the posterior application of superior force."

"Trust in the Lord with all your heart and lean not on your own understanding; in all your ways acknowledge him, and he will make your paths straight" (Proverbs 3:5-6). May the Lord give you His own peace, and the wisdom you need each day as you turn to Him for help.

How to Be a Good Mother-in-Law

1. Thank God for this acquired son or daughter.
2. Treat this man and woman as adults with adult responsibility.
3. Remember your daughter or son now belongs to her or his spouse.
4. Allow them to form a new family—it's theirs, not yours now!
5. Expect this new entity to be different from you and your family.
6. Let the newly formed family do things its own way.
7. Do not dish out gratuitous advice (which is what I'm doing now!)
8. Pray for them daily.
9. Never criticize the "in-law" to his or her spouse.
10. Encourage them in every way you can think of.

SEVEN

∾

MISSIONARY STORIES

Ecuador Journey

It had been thirty-one years since my missionary work in Ecuador had ended, and I so wanted my third husband, Lars, to get a glimpse of that beautiful county and the tribal people with whom I had worked. At last my hope was realized. Gene Jordan, whom I had known when he was a baby, flew Lars and me in the Mission Aviation plane to the eastern jungle. Once again I saw the glory of the high Andes, though partly swathed in clouds (and *pollution*—something new), the velvet mountainsides and green valleys, the great canyon of the roaring Pastaza River. Sweet memories overwhelmed me.

We landed in Tonampade, a settlement on the Curarary River where a number of Aucas (now known as *Waorani*) live. It was pouring rain, but dozens of Indians, soaked and muddy, waited on the airstrip to greet us. Dayuma was the only one I recognized. My Auca is much rustier than my Quichua, so I was glad for the help of an Auca woman married to a Quichua, who speaks both languages. She led the way to the river. It took a bit of persuading to get Lars to take off shoes and socks and roll up his trousers. I don't believe he'd ever done that in his life, but neither had he slogged through *that* kind of mud before. Of course, he had things like snakes and fire ants and scorpions in mind.

Our guide pointed out where "Palm Beach" used to be, where my first husband, Jim, and four others were killed in 1956. Because the course of jungle rivers changes so drastically, the bodies of the men were long since washed downriver, but shortly before we made our visit the Indians had found parts of Nate Saint's plane, uncovered after all these years by those capricious currents. I had found a piece of it in 1959 when two of the men who had done the spearing took Valerie and me to the beach. They told me at that time that the graves were gone. A bronze plaque, placed years later by visitors from the U.S. on what was supposed to be Palm Beach, has been washed away. A replacement now stands far from the river.

Everything was different, totally different from what it had been in Tiwaenu, many hours' travel from there and inaccessible by plane, where Valerie and I had lived. There are Christians in Tonampade. The New Testament has been translated and there is a church building, also electricity, a spigot with running water, short wave radios, houses with walls, floors, and aluminum roofs. With the introduction of paper, plastic, cans, and bottles, the people have learned to litter. Population has exploded. Oil companies have built school buildings. Aucas are working for the companies, learning Spanish, organizing themselves, protesting to the government for property rights. One time, a delegation was sent to Washington, D.C., hoping to speak to the president (who was not available).

The next day we were *driven* to Shandia. Yes, what used to be our airstrip is now a road. We made a stop in Pano *en route*, where a church service was in progress. I was asked to give "a little word," and there were tears and testimonies of Jim's influence. Venancio, the godly man who was the strongest of the Christians, and our school teacher and first pastor of the Shandia church, now lives in Pano. He was not there that day, but I had a letter from him telling of his huge disappointment knowing we would be passing through. He was preaching in a nearby town that day.

"My wife, Ana, and I could not stop crying," he wrote. "If only we had known! I always remember Shandia, and we have continued to work without ceasing for the Lord, encouraging the believers. But Satan has entered and has caused the fall of many, and many divisions, a very sad thing.... In November I and my pupils went to lay a floral offering at the grave of the five brothers. I cried much, thinking to myself, Don Jaimie and Don Eduardo and Don Pedro taught me the Bible."

At last we reached Shandia, the Quichua station where Jim and Pete Fleming worked before either was married. Word had been sent that we were coming and twenty or thirty people waited in the pouring rain in front of the Jim Elliot School, using banana leaves for umbrellas. We were greeted with a loud, warm welcome, everyone talking at once, some doing the death wail (the custom for when one sees someone he hadn't seen since a loved one died). Then we were taken to a nearby house where a man had a badly swollen foot, pierced by a palm thorn. We left our shoes there, waded down the trail toward the Atun Yacu (Big River) and through the forest to the house Jim built.

The Grifas, a large extended family, had moved in when the last missionaries moved out. An earthquake damaged our beautiful stone fireplace, so the Indians cook in a lean-to outdoors now. All the furniture except two beds is gone, screens are down, doors and drawers of kitchen built-ins are gone, bathroom sink and toilet are smashed, and everything is filthy, but never mind—the Grifas were grateful for a good roof, wood walls, and a cement floor. Lars wanted to know about everything—the room where I had written *Shadow of the Almighty,* the place where we dispensed worm medicine and injected penicillin, Valerie's bedroom, the shelf where the short-wave radio was when I got word that Jim was missing, the front door Jim went out of for the last time (and when he slammed it, I wondered if the thought had crossed his mind that he might not be back). I had continued to live there from 1956 to 1963, except for two years with the Aucas. (Could I ever have imagined I would come back with a *third* husband?)

The jungle has grown up so that the park-like surroundings of our house, its pineapple, coffee, and cocoa plantations, its palm, banana, avocado, and grapefruit trees, and the sweeping view of the Atun Yacu, are all obliterated.

While everybody stood (there was nothing to sit on) in the living room I was treated to a long, impassioned speech by Shilvi, head of the clan, about all the things that had happened since I left, most of it very sorrowful and confusing—feuds among the clans, contention in church and school, deaths, changes of all kinds. The words of a hymn came to mind, "Change and decay in all around I see—O Thou who changest not, abide with me."

Suddenly there was a terrible scream followed by a crash. A woman had collapsed. Three men dived to grab her and hold her down. I was told she has seizures when she's emotionally upset. It was a strange, almost surreal, scene—dark thunderclouds, the roar of the rain on the aluminum, the distress on the faces that surrounded me, hands touching me, earnest pleas for Lars and me to come back and stay, promises that everything would then be fixed. This was a strong tug at my heart. How I loved Shandia, that house, those dear people. Wouldn't it be lovely for Lars and me simply to pull up stakes and go there to stay?

When in the early 1960s it began to appear to me that the Shepherd was perhaps about to terminate what I had surely thought was a life's calling to Bible translation work I found it hard to accept. Was this a notion of the enemy to persuade me to look back when I had put hand to the plough? Questions tormented me for a while. The lessons of trust and patient waiting *on God* are hard, at least for one who loves to plan ahead, make decisions, and stick with them. But, in the words of a Portuguese proverb, "God writes straight with crooked lines," and He is far more interested in our getting where He wants us to be than we are in getting there. He does not discuss things with us. He *leads* us faithfully and plainly as we trust Him and simply do the next thing.

Notes From the Jungle

From time to time I am asked about those years with the Auca Indians, the tribe who, in 1956, had killed my husband Jim Elliot and four other men. The first year is described in my book *The Savage My Kinsman,* but perhaps some readers would like a glimpse into the second year. One day in August of 1958 I settled down with my notebook to do some linguistic work with a woman named Dayuma who spoke Quichua and Auca. I could converse with her in Quichua, the tribe in which I had formerly lived, but my Auca was not fluent. Here's an excerpt from my journal:

"The work which goes into this sort of thing is just gigantic for one so dull of hearing as I discover myself to be. Last week I made forty minutes' worth of tape. It took me from Monday afternoon till Friday night to transcribe without Dayuma's help. This morning I had a couple of hours with her. In that time we got through about five minutes of tape recording. Her attention is drawn to the fish that is smoking over the fire, or the stable fly that is biting Mintaka's derriere. So I play it again, make another stab at transcribing it. If the word I am trying to get happens to be one which Mintaka or Mankamu just said, I ask Dayuma what it means, but nine times out of ten, before she can give me a translation, she had to consult them. It goes something like this:

I: What does *uwiyeki* mean?

D: (knitting her brow): *Uwiyeki. Uwiyeki. Mintaka!* There's a fly biting your ankle! Get it! No, there.

Yes—oh, it got away … Uh, what did you say?

I: What does *uwiyeki* mean?

D: *Uwiyeki.* Mankamu, what did you say about *uwiyeki?* Mankamu says nothing. Mintaka answers: "We were all in the yucca patch, hiding from Muipa and his bunch. It was raining and my sister was lying in a hammock with a leaf over the baby. The water was dripping *pita pita pita pita* under the hammock. Unime always said it was better to lie in a hammock even if you got wet. Snakes couldn't bite you there at night. So while we were there in the yucca patch Dabu arrived. He said that he had come over the hill, and the others came by way of the river.

D: (translates all of the above into Quichua for me with a few interpolations of her own—none of it relevant to my question!)

I: Yes. Thank you. And what did you say *uwiyeki* means?

D: *Uwiyeki. Uwiyeki.* Mintaka! Did you say Dabu came over the hill or went by the river?

M: Nimonga and his bunch went by the river.

D: It was Dabu who came over the hill.

I: Oh. And—*uwiyeki?* What does that mean?

D: It means up and around and through the forest and over the hill, instead of through the river or by the beaches.

I: (groan, sigh) Oh.

So all *that* was what *uwiyeki* meant? To others was given the privilege over the following decades to translate the New Testament for that tribe. When Lars and I visited them in 1996 they were pleased to show us their copies.

Jungle Journey

On January 8, 1996, Lars and I along with daughter Valerie, her husband, Walt, and their eighteen-year-old son, Walter III, went back to the Curaray River in the eastern rain forest of Ecuador to visit with the Aucas (now called Waorani).

Our host was Steve Saint, son of missionary pilot Nate who was one of five men slain on that same river on January 8, 1956. Steve and his lovely wife, Ginny, had, in the space of six months, built a small village which includes their spacious three-bedroom house and a number of palm-thatched Indian houses clustered around.

The Saints' house, open all hours of the day and night for Waorani visitors, has a living room furnished with hammocks where we sat for hours and hours, talking, laughing, singing, reminiscing.

"Gikari!" they shouted using my tribal name, "you are OLD!"

"Yes," said I, "*pikyamu imupa!* I am certainly old—and so are *you!*" Great guffaws, vigourous nodding assent: *"Munitu arobainga pikyamunipa!"*

"And this is Mangari (pointing to Valerie)? Your child? She too is old! Which one is her husband? And this one here—he is her firstborn child? How many does she have?"

Then began the counting on fingers (their language has only two basic words for numbers, so fingers are necessary), endless repetitions of information for each newcomer who arrived to gaze at the old foreigners. Two of the men who had had part in the spearing of the missionaries came—Minkayi, who years ago had given me his blowgun and dart case, and Kimo, who in 1967 had gone with Rachel Saint, Nate's wife, to a worldwide evangelical congress in Berlin where he gave his testimony.

Steve asked our plans for the next day. We confessed they were not very clear. "We're going to the jungle tomorrow," he said. "Why don't we go together?" We did. In a borrowed van we traveled up to the high grass country of the Andes, through Pifo and Papallacta ("Potato Town"), down through Baeza to jungle country and what used to be the very small town of Tena. Venancio, with whom I had been corresponding for six months in order to arrange to see him and the other Quichuas I know, lives near Tena. I fully expected to find him easily. What was my dismay then to find that Tena is now a metropolis.

We stopped at a small restaurant. A young man came up to the van. *"Buenos dias,"* said he. *"Buenos dias,"* said I. *"Runa shimira rimacchu angui?"* said I, which meant, "Are you a speaker of Quichua?" (My Quichua is not quite so rusty as my Spanish.) An astonished smile spread over his face. *"Ari!"* Yes! And did he happen to know Venancio? Yes. Could he lead us to his house? Of course. Venancio's dear wife Ana fell into my arms with tears of joy, then the stunning announcement that Venancio had gone that morning to the hospital in Quito—"a ball in his neck." Alas. It sounded serious. "But he will be back this evening." We did not believe her—a five-hour bus trip each way, a visit to the doctor, etc.? No, he couldn't possibly make it.

Next questions: Where could five "gringos" spend the night?

Eduardo, our guide, knew the perfect place—at his father-in-law's. Clemente Chimbo was just a boy when I left Ecuador in 1963, but now he broadcasts the gospel in Quichua on the jungle network, and has established a little "resort"—four palm-thatched huts on the beautiful Pano River. Never had I anticipated anything nearly so luxurious, not in the jungle. A hammock, perhaps, somewhere—but beds? mattresses? sheets? blankets? pillows? *mosquito nets?* They had everything, including a pet monkey and parrot to entertain us, a little girl who raced up a tree and brought down what they called grapes, and a sort of "sitting room"—a thatched roof on poles with no walls, but benches, hammocks, and a fire. We made ourselves at home.

Clemente's wife Juanita began to cry as soon as she saw Valerie. She remembered her! They were eight years old when they last saw each other. I had forgotten her but she remembered the dolls they played with, the little playhouse which collapsed because of termites, and the fun they had in the river. On and on she went laughing and crying, hugging her friend.

But now—what would we like for supper? What did they have? Everything, they said, could be had in Tena. Everything? Well, vegetables then, please. And off they went, returning with two enormous sacks full. Juanita and her daughter-in-law soon called us to the "dining room." We ate our fill, and then sat around the fire, listening to Clemente's stories until—incredibly—Venancio suddenly appeared. He had left for Quito at 1:00 A.M. and was back. He had been the schoolteacher and Jim Elliot's right-hand man in Shandia, the Quichua station where we lived. Never did a man grieve more than Venancio did when, a few days after January 8, 1956, I returned to Shandia with the news that Jim and Ed and Pete, all of whom had worked there, and Nate who served the station with his little plane, had been killed. He had immediately taken up the "mantle," as it were, and become the shepherd of the flock of fifty newly baptized Quichua believers. I have never known a humbler, more faithful, godly man. In recent years he has been working with the Waorani also, learning their language, assisting the missionaries as he is able.

That night it rained as it can only rain in the rain forest—a tremendous battering of our thatched roofs, surely as loud as rain on palm leaves could ever be. But no—the volume gets turned up louder. And louder yet, when the Lord "tip[s] over the water jars of the heavens" (Job 38:37). Will that flimsy thatch give way? It doesn't. Indians know how to thatch roofs that last for years. But my, didn't it rain, and wasn't I delighted that we were being treated to the works! (Getting to the outhouse and down to the river to shave and wash and brush teeth—what fun for all!)

We boarded a bus that morning for the fifteen-minute ride (a three-hour walk, as I remembered it) to Shandia. The bus was packed, and as one woman moved to give Valerie a seat she suddenly cried, "I *know* you! We used to play together! Remember the playhouse that collapsed one night?" Thirty-three years had passed, yet they knew each other.

We got off the bus at the end of what used to be our airstrip, now a road, and walked to Atun Yacu (Big River), along the cliff, and through the forest to the house Jim built, where we were welcomed by the Grifa family who live there. Of course Val showed Walt and Walter though the house—her schoolroom, the guest room, her bedroom and mine, where I had written *Shadow of the Almighty* at the desk Jim had built in the corner. Then upstairs, where I taught Quichua girls to read, write, and sew. The Grifas fixed us a lunch of manioc, boiled eggs, and chichi, a drink made from manioc.

While we were sitting up there, up the trail came an Indian followed by a tall, blond, young man wearing a very fancy motorcycle suit. He came in, spoke to Walt and Lars in English with a foreign accent, then came toward me with hand outstretched.

"I know you," he said, "I've read your books in German."

I gasped. He had been studying Spanish in Quito for some time, but was determined to make a trip to Shandia to see the house Jim built, for his testimony had made a profound impact on this man's life. So he had ridden his motorcycle for five hours. Unbelievable that, in the short time we were there, this dedicated "fan" of Jim's should arrive and find Jim's wife and daughter in that house! Have we not a faithful—and amazing—Shepherd?

We had another night in our little huts, flagged a pickup truck the next morning and went to church in Tena with Venancio and Ana. We were then picked up by a Mission Aviation pilot and flown to the home of Steve and Ginny Saint on the Curarary, downriver from where the five men were killed in 1956. What a reunion with my Auca friends—many of whom are now Christians—Ipa, who was a great help to me when I was first learning the language, and many others.

Walt, Walter, and Lars were eager for a jungle trek. I bowed out. Five hours on a jungle trail? Mud? Ravines? Rainstorms? And lots of et ceteras? I'd *been* there, *done* that! Steve flew them to another airstrip, and accompanied by an Indian and Steve's son Jess, they slogged five hours thorough the forest, most of the time in a state-of-the-art downpour. Lovely. The full treatment, the works, again, and nary a syllable of complaint from one of them.

Ginny served us, in addition to more familiar things, wild turkey, wild pig, and woolly monkey, brought by one of the hunters. In the evening a great crowd filled all the hammocks in the house—school children and their teacher, proud parents who couldn't read but were thrilled that their children could. They recited and sang for us, and some of the old men and women sang their ancient traditional three-note songs (I remembered one of them and sang along). Then we *kurwuri* (foreigners) were commanded to perform as well. We obliged, with old gospel songs (in English, of course) and even some childhood songs with motions—"Climb, Climb Up Sunshine Mountain," etc. No one wanted to leave. It was far past bedtime for us old folks, but who could leave such joyful company? Who could bear to miss hearing Kimo and Minkayi, two of the men who had part in the massacre, pray, thinking God for sending Jesus to teach them how to live, asking Him to help them to love Him more?

Letter From a Missionary

(From Dr. Steve Hawthorne, of Potosi, Bolivia, a nephew of Jim Elliot)

I hate to admit it because altruistic missionary doctors shouldn't be prejudiced. But the fact is my heart sank when I saw the tiny figure. At least her cataracts kept her from seeing the dismay my face must have registered at the appearance of yet another Little Old Quechua Lady that morning. As she stood in the doorway and clapped her hands to announce her presence it wasn't just my preference for pediatrics and obstetrics versus geriatrics that made me sigh. I dreaded the difficulty we would have communicating. She would not speak one word of Spanish and her Quechua words would be blurred by not having any teeth left. She would likely be deaf and my shouted replies would serve only to entertain the listeners in the waiting room. I guessed that whatever problem she had was not amenable to any therapy I could offer. Probably it was advanced osteo-arthritis of her knees from chasing goats over the mountains for seventy years; or loss of hearing and vision; or weakness from not being able to chew nutritious food for lack of teeth; or chronic constipation from Chagas' disease and binding her abdomen with petticoats. Finally, if I did have some medicine to offer her, she was not likely to have any money to pay for it. Suppressing a fleeting thought of escape through the open window, I beckoned her in.

"She entered with a bent-over, painful gait, leaning on a stick. Over her shoulder was a blanket handwoven of black wool, carrying a branch she had collected on the way for her evening cooking fire. Her face was deeply seamed, the eyes rheumy, the fingers that grasped the stick were twisted sideways. Her fedora hat had years since lost its shape; her skirt announced that it had been lived and slept in for days unnumbered. Encased in rubber sandals her dusty feet were callused, the nails thickened. But she had not completely neglected her appearance: her two braids (which are a Quechua woman's pride) were short, thin, and gray, but I noticed she had augmented them with black yarn.

"She didn't know her age so I put it down as seventy-five. All my little Quechua Ladies are recorded as seventy-five. She was a widow and lived alone, as her children had long since left the mountains for the city. She had many aches and pains and as I cradled her knee in my hands I could feel the crepitations when she moved her leg. As I examined her I remembered how in the elderly, long after vision and hearing have been lost, the sense of touch is preserved, and I hoped that something of the love of God could flow through my palms to warm the worn-out joint beneath.

"I was right about her not having any money to pay for the analgesics I gave her, and she had many questions about what foods she should and shouldn't eat and whether or not it was OK to touch water. I finally brought the interview to a close, anxious to get on to the next person waiting. She was not through, however, and I paced impatiently as she unpinned the knot of the blanket on her back and began unfolding it, every movement painstakingly slow and deliberate. She reached into the depths and withdrew two small eggs, which she pressed into my hand—her widow's mite. Then she made her way cautiously out, leaning on her stick, leaving me with an epiphany: 'Pure and lasting religion in the sight of God our Father means that we must care for orphans and widows in their troubles' (James 1:27)."

Travels

*B*eijing: a little yearly retreat with American women who work in China. Spoke to various groups, once in the university, and once in a very tiny, cramped apartment for a few students who courageously have come to Christ—a charming, happy crew, their lives so recently transformed. Lars watched a huge slaughtered animal being de-furred outside a restaurant that advertised dog as its specialty. He decided against eating there.

We had never been to China before. Its vastness, its teeming millions, its industry overwhelmed me. So it exists? There really is a place called China? I thought of the hymn sung to the tune of Londonderry Air, "I cannot tell how He will win the nations, how we will claim His earthly heritage, how to satisfy the needs and aspirations of East and West, of sinner and of sage. But this I know, all flesh shall see His glory, and He shall reap the harvest He has sown, and some glad day His sun will shine in splendor when He the Savior, Savior of the world is known."

Mongolia: a thirty-hour train trip out of Beijing, past the Great Wall which climbs needle-sharp peaks; past where coolies were working on a superhighway using hand tools, cutting stone, carting dirt in wheelbarrows, digging tunnels; past little villages, mud-brick houses and outdoor ovens, nuclear plants and coal heaps, green grass country like the high Andes, horses drinking from a stream, shepherd with flocks, rice paddies with squatting figures at work.

At 9:00 P.M. the train empties at the border of Mongolia. The wheels must be changed to a narrower gauge. We fill out papers, passports are examined again and again, five hours later we board and go to bed. A knock on the door demands papers and passports—*again*. We are searched and questioned, an exercise in futility, as no one speaks English! To bed again, another knock, two officials scratch heads over what to do with us, and finally give up.

By 8:45 A.M., we've seen horses, cows, goats, dogs, camels, and one small deer or antelope. We are crossing the vast Gobi Desert, familiar to me because as a child I had read of Mildred Cable and Francesca French, those two dauntless missionaries who crossed it (but not by train). We stop in a town where little boys beg for handouts. We toss out cookies and pens. They pounce on them and tear away. Later we are excited to see a herd of dromedaries close to the railroad.

We are met at the Ulaan Bataar station by Martha Taylor, a six-feet-two, gracious, and lovely Southern Baptist, and her driver, to whom she spoke the most impossibly difficult-sounding language I've ever heard. Supper with a Christian Mongolian family: meat turnovers, cabbage, and carrot salad.

I spoke to earnest young people in a Bible school. They prayed simultaneously with great fervor and listened intently. A beautiful drive out of the city into great rolling hills, green grass, weird rock formations. A visit to a *ger* (*yurt* in Russian)—a round house like a cake, built with wooden slats covered with skins, then with felt (which Mongolians invented, they said), then with white canvas. All are alike, about twenty feet in diameter with a stove in the center, a hole in the roof. They were friends of Martha, and although they were not expecting us, they immediately set about fixing food: very weak tea with hot milk and *salt*, yogurt, boiled lamb and strange hard slabs of butter that doesn't melt. Mongolians as a rule eat nothing but meat and milk. "Animals eat vegetables," they explain, "We eat the animals." There were brightly painted wooden beds and cupboards, a very adequate and simple life—and in such magnificent surroundings.

Back to the city, tea with a group of sweet Christian Mongol girls, other meetings including a weekend retreat for expatriates, then a flight back to Beijing.

Supper in a restaurant where no one spoke English. Huge hilarity. We managed to get chicken with peanuts and boiled fish by using appropriate gestures that had the whole staff in stitches. Flying home, I woke to a breathtaking wrinkled no-man's land (Siberia?)—brown earth spotted with frozen puddles, snow-covered mountains stretching to the far horizon, and black rivers snaking through all. Not a sign of humanity.

I was keenly aware of my utter dependence on the Lord, a "being sheltered" by Him, and remembered a hymn my mother loved to sing: "All the way my Savior leads me, what have I to ask beside?"

The Simple Life

The Dohnavur Fellowship, the work Amy Carmichael started in South India, is always on my heart. I want to do all I can to remind you that it still goes on. Neither I nor anyone else is authorized to solicit funds for the DF, but I am allowed to give you a glimpse of the sort of place it is.

Margaret Holland wrote in *Dust of Gold*, the DF prayer letter, of how they continue to cling to "the simple life" because it usually costs less, and "we have a duty to our friends, who give often sacrificially, to be good stewards of all that we have. Many things available to us now are not wrong in themselves but are not necessities, and we have always wanted the Family to grow up free from the deception of materialism and able to find their joy and satisfaction in life from all the good things the Lord has given us so freely, both in the spiritual realm and in the natural world around us. Many of our sisters have gone out to jobs or marriage in a rural environment where, for economic and social reasons, life has remained simple and conservative. For them it is essential that they should know how to grind their own flour by hand, cook over a wood fire, and be used to hard physical work.

"Gradually, as people have begun to enjoy better incomes and an improved standard of living as a result, the world around is changing and so is the answer to the question, 'What is the simple life?' Some changes have been adopted of necessity, for example, the changeover to gas from firewood for cooking purposes, although the old stoves are still used for some things. Shortage, the poor quality of firewood, and ever-increasing prices were major factors, together with an awareness of the damage to the environment as wood-cutters made ever-deeper inroads into the foothill forest to cut green wood.... Other areas of improvement: installation of an electric wet-grinder for the preparation of rice-flour for breakfast food. This was done formerly in the evening using granite pestles and mortars sunk into the kitchen floor.

"It was quite an innovation when about six transistor radios were introduced about twenty years ago and circulated 'round the compounds in turn so that people could listen to the news!... Not all have very good discretion when it comes to choice of programmes, but there is a limit to the extent to which rules and regulations can be laid down governing every aspect of life. Developing a sense of personal responsibility would seem to be the profitable way....

"For many years a holiday highlight was the wildlife and documentary reel-films loaned out by the various High Commissions. A few years ago these were replaced by videos and so it seemed the time had come to buy a TV and a video recorder, and also to take advantage of the same kind of BBC programmes obtainable by satellite; hence the satellite dish located in the field between the kindergarten and the clock tower!

"While our hospital retains its simplicity, it is nevertheless the 'Place of Heavenly Healing,' where prayer and medicine are practiced together. However, our three dental surgeries are equipped with the most modern equipment which compares favourably with any well-equipped practice in the West." She goes on to mention telephones, a fax machine, and—to help with editing and mailing of *Dust of Gold*—a computer is being considered.

"Some of you, whilst reading the above, may be amused to think that we should even bother to write about such things, when they have been taken for granted as part of everyday life in the West for so long. But perhaps that is what most underlines what tremendous changes are taking place in rural India, which is struggling to catch up not just with the West, but with modern India itself.

"What is the simple life? Obviously it is made up of different things for different people. Perhaps one way of looking at it might be to say that anything which works for the common good in a community may have a rightful place without increasing 'clutter' and materialism. The danger comes when, in our personal lives, we feel we need to possess everything that is available just because it's there, or for prestige or self-indulgence. To make do with less, or the lesser, will mean, for most of us, that we have more to share with others whose basic spiritual and material needs are unmet. We cannot generalize; but each one of us does have the responsibility both personally and corporately to be faithful stewards of what God has entrusted to us, and to live in the spirit of the Scripture verse, 'Do not love the world or anything in the world.' We have Someone far more worthy of our love—'the Giver of every good and perfect gift.'"

"O Thou, whose name is Love, Who never turnest away from the cry of Thy needy children, give ear to my prayer this morning. Make this

a day of blessing to me, and make me a blessing to others. Keep all evil away from me. Preserve me from outward transgression and from secret sin. Help me to control my temper. May I check the first risings of anger or sullenness. If I meet with unkindness or ill-treatment, give me that charity which suffereth long and beareth all things. Make me kind and gentle towards all, loving even those who love me not. Let me live this day as if it were to be my last. O my God, show me the path that Thou wouldest have me to follow. May I take no step that is not ordered by Thee, and go nowhere except Thou, Lord, go with me. Amen." (Aston Drenden)

An Unusual Christmas Celebration

*F*oreigners help for limited times at the Dohnavur Fellow-ship, but an Indian woman, Nesaruthina Carunia, is the director. All her regular staff are Indian. In the beautiful compound there is a hospital where at Christmastime a feast is given for the lepers—a feast very different from American celebrations, yet one which surely means infinitely more to those sufferers than our elaborate expensive ones. As I read Balaleela's account in the prayer letter, *Dust of Gold*, I thought what a prodigious undertaking it is, yet how full of deep joy both for the guests and for those who work so hard to prepare everything. Ponder the relative simplicity of the occasion, in contrast to our frantic Christmas spending and so often harried and hectic attempts to "have fun." Here is the story:

"'Behold, I am the Lord, the God of all flesh; is there anything too hard for Me?'" (Jeremiah 32:27).

"'Always pray and never lose heart' (Luke 18:1).

"These were challenging verses to me when I was praying about the Leprosy Feast. Very few patients had been to collect medicines recently as the special drug we were given had been stopped in accordance with Government ruling. It was the rainy season and this could have prevented many from coming to the Feast, but God had everything in hand.

"Cooks were engaged, foodstuffs and vegetables, etc. were bought, cooking vessels hired. Firewood was stacked and ready and extra electric lights installed. Banana leaves, for use as plates, were washed and placed in neat piles; spoons and coconut-shell ladles counted. Hospital staff enjoyed collecting the yellow tecoma flowers to make into garlands and the whole place was decorated with colored stars, etc.

"The night of cooking started with prayer, then the employees washed and chopped and cooked. The team was cheered by visits from our Accals and Annachies [the women and men who work at Dohnavur, which includes those who care for the more than four hundred children who live there.] The Lord controlled the weather, so that they were able to do most of the cooking in the outer courtyard. However, early in the morning heavy rain began, and a place had to be found for the frying under the cover of the roof.

"When it was all finished the garlands were hung, and the outpatient waiting-halls looked beautiful. The patients started to arrive and before 9:00 A.M. there were more than 150 people. We held the meeting inside the hall instead of in the open air and the people listened attentively. The speaker had a profound message for the patients as well as for those helping them. Heaps of rice and curry were served and they happily started to fill up their vessels also, to take home for other family members! Although it is the custom in India to eat with the fingers, some guests needed spoons because their fingers were too deformed or missing altogether.

"Each guest was given a Christmas card with a Tamil Bible text added, a banana, and the children also had a flower posy to decorate their hair. They all seemed very happy.

"After the Feast, those who needed medicines collected them and set off for home. As soon as they had left it started to pour rain, which made their journey difficult but made our job of cleaning up much easier. The remaining food was distributed among the employees who had worked all night and those who had helped clear up afterwards.

"The Lord helped us to pray and not lose heart, and our reward was to see so many patients come. Praise and glory to God for whom nothing is too hard."

Pray for India

*O*ne year in May, we were invited to Pollachi for the annual conference of the Women's Prayer Fellowship of South India. Four hundred women sitting cross-legged on a cement floor for hours at a time, backs straight, faces lifted heavenward, is a scene which will always be with me. They were, one and all, dressed in saris, that most beautifully feminine of all women's costumes. (They asked me to wear one when I spoke. It took fifteen minutes of expert winding, pleating, and wrapping to dress me. A sari is one piece of fabric, eighteen feet long.)

They were there for four days, sleeping on a cement floor, the day beginning with a prayer meeting at 4:30 A.M. and continuing until 10:00 or 11:00 P.M. when supper was served (on the days they did not fast). I spoke, of course, by interpretation, marveling that they did not seem bored or restless but gazed at this pale-faced stranger with eager smiles and warm sympathy.

Our two hostesses throughout the trip were Princess, who is 27, and Daisy, 26—both missionaries to tribespeople in the north. One of those groups, the Malto, numbers 100,000, and there are 35,000 Christians. I was astounded to learn that there are 4,653 different tribes or "people groups" in India, forty of which still practice human sacrifice. There are 1,652 languages in India, only 49 of which have the whole Bible; 46 have the New Testament. Do pray for them, and for precious little Princess and Daisy, whose lifestyle is perhaps the most sacrificial I have ever heard of in missionary work. They illustrate Ugo Bassi's oft-quoted words:

Measure thy life by loss and not by gain;
Not by the wine drunk but by the wine poured
　forth,
For love's strength standeth in love's sacrifice,
And he that suffereth most hath most to give.

The eternal God is your refuge,
And underneath are the everlasting arms.

DEUTERONOMY 33:27

Other Books by Elisabeth Elliot

Keep a Quiet Heart
(companion volume to *Secure in the Everlasting Arms*)

A Lamp for My Feet

The Liberty of Obedience

Love Has a Price Tag

The Music of His Promises

The Path of Loneliness

A Path Through Suffering

The Savage My Kinsman

These Strange Ashes

AVAILABLE AT YOUR LOCAL CHRISTIAN BOOKSTORE
AND WHEREEVER BOOKS ARE SOLD